ISLAM
IN MODERN WORLD

ABUBAKAR YARO (KHALIFA) PHD DSC MSC

authorHOUSE®

AuthorHouse™ UK
1663 Liberty Drive
Bloomington, IN 47403 USA
www.authorhouse.co.uk
Phone: UK TFN: 0800 0148641 (Toll Free inside the UK)
UK Local: (02) 0369 56322 (+44 20 3695 6322 from outside the UK)

Published by AuthorHouse 10/26/2024

ISBN: 979-8-8230-8894-7 (sc)
ISBN: 979-8-8230-8893-0 (e)

Special thanks to the Publishing Team for making this book a possibility AND to my family for bearing the brunt of my academic journey!

First edition:

IN THE NAME OF ALLAH

The Most Gracious, the Most Merciful
"And We have sent you (O Muhammad SAW) not but as a
mercy for the alamin (mankind, jinns, and all that exits)
(21: 107)

CONTENTS

Preface xi

Acknowledgement.. xiii

The Beginning.. 1

The Religion of Knowledge... 13

Zakat-the best form of donation for ending poverty 31

A Disunited People (Muslims)... 39

Modern Events that impacted Islam & Lessons from them 50

Jesus (AS) of Islam 56

Islam, the Pan-global religion: Hope for the world 64

Ethics and Morality of the Quran 70

References 83

PREFACE

Islam is a religion whose foundation is built on peace yet it is the most misunderstood religion in the world. The western media has given the religion so much bad publicity that when you ask even the most advanced academic non-Muslim about Islam; he/she will not even have anything good about the religion to say. I have this good Christian friend who always complains that how can I be associating myself with a religion that promotes suppression of women and killings? I always look surprised because she is well educated. Two misconceptions that have been associated with Islam are jihad and polygamy. Apart from these misconceptions, within the Muslim community itself there is totally disunity that makes one marvels at what is happening to a people whose Prophet (SAW) was the most tolerant and promoted unity among the Muslim community? He (SAW) once advised Muslims that "Muslims are brothers and sisters who should stay together". Another time, he (SAW) predicted to his companions (RA) a time will come that the Muslim community will be so disunited that they can't fight their enemies. He (SAW) was asked: "***Will they be few in numbers***"? He (SAW) responded: "***They will be large in numbers but disunity will be their downfall***" (My words).

The current predicament of Muslims is so sad and pathetic which requires urgent call for Muslims to go back to the basics of Islam. One story I found very inspiring was a story of one companion who cooked meat but when he was about to eat, he asked himself whether the Prophet (SAW) has eaten so sent the cooked meat to the Prophet (SAW). The Prophet (SAW) in turn sent to another companion. That meat was circulated till it came back to the Prophet (SAW). He (SAW) had to bring all those involved for them to eat together. This is the power and beauty of unity! But in the present generation, Muslims have become so greedy, selfish and disunited to the extent that that sense of pride and unity are gone. I remember one convert who said: "If I had examined Muslims first, I wouldn't have come to the religion." He said the truth! In this must read book, I delve into Islam from a Scientific perspective and as a proud Muslim. This means my conclusions to the texts that I read may not be perfect during my synthesis! The Prophet (SAW) once remarked that every 100 years a reformer will be sent to reform the religion (Islam). This reformer maybe an individual, groups, or country. May we be the reformers who will fight for Islam (Amen).

I attempt to utilize my knowledge as a scientist to address some pressing issues confronting Islam and Muslims. This book is written in simple language so that it can reach very large audience. That doesn't make me the best in synthesis of data among Muslims and other scholars. What I present in this publication is the result of intensive research. May Allah (SWT) grant us the wisdom, strength and passion to follow the teachings of the greatest human being to grace this world (SAW) and May Allah forgive me for any wrong interpretation in this book (Amen).

ACKNOWLEDGEMENT

My first gratitude goes to My Creator (SWT) who has being my protector and guider. Everything I have being able to achieve are through the Mercies of Allah (SWT). My next thanks go to my parents: Alhaji Abdullah Yaro (father) and Amina Ahmed (mother) for not only been excellent parents to me but also been source my of inspiration. My children are always on the sacrificial side of my academic and research duties. Thanks for understanding me and giving me both the moral and religious support as I try to fulfil my duties as a Scientist and an academician. What I have been able to achieve would not have been possible without worldly assistance that was provided perfectly by my teachers from my primary education through my university education and beyond the corridor of learning. I thank all these gallant men and women who had hard time channelling my anger to something fruitful. I cannot forget to mention my academic friends and colleagues such as Professor Ashok Rattan, Professor Pranab Bhattacharya, and all staffs at AHRO Network, etc who were always there with me. On social media, I always respect the views of Chikakay for she is really pointing the present generation to the path of truth. Although she always claims she is not a scholar, I do learn a lot from her. To my wives Memuna Habib and Hajara Gambaga, thanks so much for being my source of happiness.

THE BEGINNING

━━━━━━━━━━━ ❖ ━━━━━━━━━━━

Many have asked the question: Why Islam? Before this question is answered, let us recap the state of the world before Islam. This is the period referred to as "Jahiliyya". The word is used to characterize the period before the coming of the Prophet of Islam (SAW). In English language it means period of ignorance. In the pre-Islamic Arabian Peninsula, the dominant religion was the Bedouin polytheists. They didn't believe in one God and they believed that man should worship a God through intermediary such as tree or stones. There were other religions such as Judaism consisting of several clans. In some places such as Yemen, there was Christians with monks and hermits. They consisted of people with varying understanding of who Jesus (AS) was; with some believing he (AS) was son of God while others believed he (AS) was a messenger of God. There were another group called the Hanifs who didn't believe in polytheism but spent their time exploring monotheistic.

The social background of the period of Jahiliyya was based on power. The Arabs were then divided on the basis of their common ancestors with tribes consisting of clans. Some of the tribes were wealthier than others. For example the Prophet (SAW) was from the tribe of Quraysh and within his tribe he (SAW) belonged to the clan known as Hashim. Because the social system was based on clans, discontent was difficult to deal with. The idea was economic challenges were addressed thorough the system of vendetta i.e. when you kill one of my clan, I will also kill one of yours or we go to war. During this period of Jahiliyya, women were of low social status and female babies were often killed at birth because they thought having a female child was a disgrace (infanticide).

Their political system was based on the rules of the Byzantine Empire. The Sassanian Empire was then ruling East of China to Iraq. Tribes are clans and each clan had a leader with such leaders having councils where tribal issues are discussed. Within the tribes, all members were loyal to the extent that killing each other was forbidden.

However, the people of Jahiliyya had some good aspect. They were generous people; they agreed that of the 12 months, there won't be war in four months. They possessed great skills in archery and horsemanship while they were of the opinion that when one flee from the country, it was absolutely unacceptable. This meant they believed in nationalism.

So what are the main features of this period of Jahiliyya?

Immorality was practiced openly and the worship of idols was the order of the day. Female infanticide was viewed as honour. This I find interesting because the human rights activists, both past and present have not given Islam the credit for fighting against female infanticides. Drunkenness, wars, usury and sexual immorality was practiced everywhere. It was in this dark period that the Prophet of Islam (SAW) was born in fulfilment of the prediction of Jesus (AS) who said "if I don't go the Holy Spirit will not come." The Holy Spirit literally means the man who possesses the spirit of God. The Prophet of Islam (SAW) in the Quran is referred to as "Rahman" meaning "Gracious" or "merciful" or "beneficent" or "the mercy-giving". These are attributes of someone possessing the spirit of God. Why is this essential? Because one of the names of Allah is also "Al-Rahman". By this he (SAW) was sent as a blessing to mankind, the Prophet (SAW) was the Holy Spirit that represented God on earth. He (SAW) is the most beloved of Allah as described by Dr Salim bin Muhammad Rafi in his book titled "Muhammad, the beloved of Allah". This world was created because of him (SAW) and the day of reckon is for him (SAW)!

It was in this moment of darkness that Muhammad (SAW) was born and later became a Prophet. Who is the man Prophet Muhammad (SAW)?

Prophet Mohammed Ibn Abdullahi (SAW)

Signs of Prophethood at the early stage of his (SAW) life

In accepting the message of Muhammad (SAW), the world is divided into four groups: the Muslims, Christians, the Jews, and the animists.

A Muslim is the person who day in day out recite the kalimatu shahada (*ašhadu ʾanna lā ilāha illa l-Lāh, wa ʾašhadu ʾanna muḥammadar rasūlu l-Lāh)* which means "I bear witness that there is no god but Allah and Muhammad (SAW) is the messenger of Allah". This is the proclamation that brings an individual to Islam and any person who believes and recite this accepts that Prophet Muhammad (SAW) is messenger of Allah. Anyone not accepting this proclamation is not a Muslim.

Almost on daily basis, Muslims have to be answering the same questions over and over: Is Muhammad (SAW) a real prophet of God? Which is related to how Islam was propagated with Muslims also trying to answer the misinformation that Muhammad (SAW) spread Islam through the power of sword? Then the so-called human right activists also blatantly accusing the Holy Prophet (SAW) of being the source of downgrading of women. For many years, these questions are refusing to go even in this era where information is at the tip of everyone's finger. The Prophet (SAW) once predicted:

> *"A time would come when people of that generation would have information readily by the finger tip."* This was a prediction of the era of advanced technology that we are now witnessing.

In a write-up posted on Wikipedia titled Medieval Christians view on Muhammad, it was written*: "Various Western and Byzantine Christians thinkers considered Muhammad to be a perverted, deplorable mans, a false prophet, and even the Antichrist, as he was frequently seen in Christendom as a heretic or possessed by demons."* Are these descriptions of Muhammad (SAW) true? In every circumstance before any issue is discussed, it is best to start with the foundation of that issue. The foundation of Islam is Prophet Muhammad (SAW). As a scientist, I was trained to analyze data and draw conclusions out of that data. Today, I am a Muslim not because I met my parents been Muslims but at a time I decided to research Islam and other religions. After intensive period of research, I came to the conclusion that Islam is the religion of truth.

Who is the man Prophet Muhammad (SAW)? I am going to analyze him (SAW) based on concise analysis of the message he (SAW) conveyed to the world. On his (SAW) last pilgrimage he (SAW) asked:

> *"Have I conveyed the message?"* The Muslims answered *"Yes, you have."*

Muhammad (SAW) was born in Mecca around the year 570 AD to Abdullahi and Amina. Before the birth of the prophet (SAW), an interesting event happened which need to be discussed. Abdul Muttalib was the grandfather of the prophet (SAW). One day he prayed to Allah (SWT) to bless him with ten male children and let them grow to adulthood. He promised to sacrifice one of them for Allah. During that period, it was regarded as norm. We know how the father Mary (AS) mother of Jesus (AS) who also prayed that if God gave him male child, he will dedicate her to God. Abdul Muttalib's prayer was accepted and he was blessed with ten boys. Of these boys, Abdullahi was the most loved and was endowed with extreme beauty. Since Abdul Muttalib was a man of his words, he decided to sacrifice one of his children. As a custom during that time, lots were casts and it fell on Abdullah. Human nature is unique in that no matter how one values integrity, it is hard to harm the one you love most. Abdul Muttalib became sad because the lots fell on Abdullah so he went to Mughirah who was the chief of Makhzum, the tribe of Fatimah, the mother of Abdullah to narrate the vow he made to Allah. Mughirah suggested that: *"Thou shalt not sacrifice Abdullah, but offer a sacrifice in his stead; it may be that his ransom be all the property of the sons of Makhzum, we shall redeem him."* Abdul Muttalib as was practiced during that time decided to consult a fortune-teller woman in Al-Medina who could tell him whether it is possible to exchange Abdullah or not. When he met her, she told him: *"Word has come to me, what is the blood money amongst you?"* He told her it is normally ten camels so she recommended that *"put your man and ten camels' side by and cast lost between them. If the arrow fell against your man, add more camels and cast lots again; and if needed add more camels until your Lord accepts them and the arrow falls against them, then sacrifice the camels and let the man lives."* The arrow kept falling against Abdullah till the camels reached one hundred, only then did the arrow fell on them. Abdul Muttalib then sacrificed hundred camels for Abdullah to live. Years later, Abdullah became the father of the greatest man to grace this world, Muhammad (SAW). What spiritual message can we derive from the scenario of casting lots between Abdullah and the camels? The answer is simple because Abdullah was to become the father of a prophet, Allah had to save him. After the marriage of Abdullah to Amina in 569 AD, Abdullah travelled to Palestine and Syria for business trip. On his way back, he fell sick and died in Al-Medina in his grandmother's family home. By then Amina was pregnant and as she recalled she heard voice telling her: *"Thou carrieth in thy womb the lord of his nation; and when he is born say: 'I place beneath the protection of the One; from the evil of every envier'; then name him Ahmed"* Weeks later, the child was born while Amina was in the house of her uncle at the time so she sent words to Abdul Muttalib, asking him to come see his grandson. Abdul Muttalib named him Muhammad (SAW) which was then an unusual name in Arabia at that time.

During that time, the act of governess was practiced in Arabia where a woman was allowed to take a child to breastfeed him/her for some time. Based on historical narration, the first governess of the Prophet (SAW) was a lady called Thuwaibah but she was soon relieved of her role. Another governess was needed; but most of the women didn't accept the Prophet (SAW) since he was an orphan. Only Halimah Sa'adiyah accepted to take him. Halima became his foster mother and her son his (SAW) foster brother.

Let's go back into history and recalled what Halimah said: *"We had no spring harvest that year as there was no rain and we had nothing to earn. I suggested to my husband that we should go to Mecca to bring a child and rear him to earn our living. My husband accepted the proposal and I along with my young baby in lap, rode the dromedary and we headed to Mecca. My child cried with hunger and there was no milk in my breast. Due to drought even the dromedary had no milk; therefore, we went hungry most of the time. When we reached Mecca, our fellow women of Banu Sa'd were returning with the children of rich people with appropriate rewards. We could not have a baby from a well-off family; instead there was only an orphan child of a family which could not reward us well. Instead of retuning empty-handed, I thought it was better to take him with us, thinking he might be able to acknowledge us when he grows up (as he belongs to the tribe of Quraysh) as a respectable man,*

5

and remember our old relationship. My husband accepted this suggestion and we began preparation to return. We had hardly covered half the distance from Mecca, when I observed to my utmost surprise that my both breast were filled with milk so much that both children had their full shares."

When we reached home, my husband pointed at the teats of the dromedary and said:

> 'Look, Halimah, they are filled with milk.' We, were weak with hunger, milked her to our heart's content. We spent that night very comfortably. Next day, my husband said to me, 'O Halimah, the child you have brought is very auspicious and he will definitely change our fortune."

What the husband didn't know was they have brought the mercy of Allah (SWT) to their house and their fortune was about to change!

Describing the Prophet (SAW), Halimah had this wonderful testimony: "He did justice right from the beginning. He sucked milk only from one side leaving the other for his foster brother Abdullah. His growth was better than any other child and he seemed bugger than his age. Everyone was struck with his innocence and charm of his personality. His face radiated like the full moon in darkness. He went out to play with other children, but would not take part in untidy activities. He was helpful and co-operative from the very beginning. At the age of three, he began to go out with his foster brother to help him graze the sheep."

The Prophet (SAW) childhood was marked with tragedies; he lost his mother and grandfather. It was his uncle Abu Talib who took care of him (SAW). Abu Talib had a large family so Muhammad (SAW) was compelled to start working to earn a living at a young age of eight years. He started taking sheep out in order to help his uncle. We need to critically analyse this phase of his life. Working at such a young age prepares one for everything that life has to offer. In the Prophet (SAW), it created a strong willpower and his intellectual capability. This was important for the mission he was entrusted upon by Allah (Prophethood). By taking the cattle to graze, the Prophet took time to mediate and ponder over life. History has shown that a child who struggled at such a young age builds his mental acumen and deep thinking is one of the traits they develop.

The desert is an ideal environment for such unique training. Psychologists have argued that a tree grown in the desert is stronger than a tree grown in other place therefore it has been opined that when a tree is plant in the desert it some fragrance to the extent that if a non-flagrant flower from other part of the world is cultivated in the desert, after some generation, it develop pleasant fragrance. The hard nature of the desert prepares the tree to become strong and able to withstand the harsh environment. Aside the effect of the desert, the Prophet (SAW) was an orphan. Nobody would like to grow up and say *"I am happy my parents died while I was a child"*. If life gives you lemon, you can change it to lemonade. In some rare cases some orphan grows up to outgrow their society through immense and rare ability to think. They mature early and build an intellectual ability that is beyond description. Because they don't have parents who would care for them, these orphans became aware of the realities of life and decided subconsciously that they would change their destiny. He/she trust only their judgement. This brave orphan must find a way to overcome any hardship confronting him/her. The burden of orphanage made the Prophet (SAW) to understand the realities of life. Based on his intellectual prowess and honesty, his uncle Abu Talib decided to include him on his trade mission to Syria.

In the early phase of his life, Halimah his foster mother gave an honest and moving testimony about his justice and radiant face. This testimony showed that the boy (SAW) was ordained for something bigger later in his (SAW) life. The next testimony would cement the argument of who was he (SAW). In one of their journeys, Abu Talib went to the city of Busra in Syria which was close of a monastery of a man called Bahirah. This hermit has never stepped out of his monastery nor has he ever had discussions with any traveller of caravans. On that day, he stepped out of his monastery and saw caravans approaching near his monastery. He then observed a small low-hanging cloud that was moving slowly above the head of the caravan. The cloud was always between the sun and one of two of the travellers. When they halted, the cloud also stopped moving, and remained stationary over the tress where they took shelter. One interesting observation he made was the trees lowered their branches over them like greeting or showing respect to the someone among the travellers. To feed his curiosity, he approached them and told them *"Men of Quraysh, I have prepared food for you"*. He then added *"Men of Quraysh, let none of you stay behind."* His reason was he wanted to see over who the cloud was. However, when the men of Quraysh were going they left Muhammad (SAW) to watch over the caravan. When they went, Bahirah didn't see the cloud so he asked them whether they brought everyone but they responded *"We left only a boy, the youngest of us all behind."* But Bahirah asked them not to treat him that way so he was asked to go in. On glancing at the boy (SAW), Bahirah immediately saw what he was looking for, between his (SAW) shoulders was the mark he was expecting to see based on the description of seal of Prophethood. Bahirah then called Abu Talib aside and told him of a dream he had: *"A caravan would come with a boy who has been commissioned by Allah to become a prophet among the Arab. Henceforth, do not be compelled to follow Judaism or Christianity as Allah is going to appoint a Prophet for you."* Bahirah then advised Abu Talib to immediately take his nephew to Mecca and protect him from the Jews. Why did Bahirah gave that suggestion? It was because the Jews were expecting the last Prophet which was given in their books. This prediction was stated in Deuteronomy 18:18 where God speaking to Moses (AS) said:

> *"I will raise them up a Prophet from among their brethren, like unto thee, and will put my words in his mouth; and he shall speak unto them all that I shall command him."*

Abu Talib took Bahirah's warning seriously and quickly completed his business mission and went back to Mecca. These narrations confirmed the Prophethood of Muhammad (SAW).

The Trustworthy Man (SAW)

Because of his trustworthiness, the people of Quraysh refer to him (SAW) as al-Amin (meaning trustworthy) before he (SAW) even became a Prophet. History books are filled with the wonderful trustworthy traits of Prophet Muhammad (SAW). Abu Dawud had this: When Muhammad (SAW) was 30 years old, a merchant promised to meet him at a place to discuss something about trading. The merchant forgot of the meeting so didn't turn up. Three days, while passing the place they were supposed to meet, the merchant saw the Prophet (SAW) standing there as he was fulfilling his (SAW) promise. Who can do this if not the Holy Prophet (SAW).

Another story worth mentioning was his encounter with a merchant named Qais bin Zaid. This Arab merchant normally gave Muhammad (SAW) his merchandise to sell at far places and upon his (SAW) return; he usually gave the merchant all the profits accrued. He could have kept this huge amount but as Al-Amin, he (SAW) always gave accurate account. This led to Qais to always pray for the Prophet (SAW): *"O Muhammad, may long life be bestowed upon you. I will never find a person more gentle and honest as you."*

His charity and trustworthiness led Imam Hanbal to write*:" Whenever Muhammad (SAW) returned from a journey, he would ask of his friends and if some were not financially sound, he would give some portion of his earnings to them in charity."*

When the Prophet (SAW) decided to migrate to Mecca, he (SAW) did something reserved only men of wisdom, justice, and fairness. Despite the harsh persecutions by the Quraysh, on the day of his (SAW) migration, he (SAW) gave the properties of the very people who were persecuting him (SAW) to his (SAW) cousin Ali ibn Talib (RA) to return to the rightful owner. These noble acts would not be spoken of by those who dislike him (SAW) but rather continue to fill their books with fake stories proclaiming that the Prophet (SAW) was an abuser of women and the sword man who used excessive force to spread the religion!

Muhammad (SAW): The supporter of the fundamental right of women

One myth which has been argued over and over again and again is the stance of the Muhammad (SAW) on women. To the western philosophers, Muhammad (SAW) was a man who took women as second class citizens and through this he (SAW) promoted the act of polygamy which to these philosophers was detrimental to the right of women. Before we elucidate the concept of polygamy and status of women from Islamic perspective, it is essential that the western views of polygamy and how women are viewed in western society are critically evaluated.

Western legal system views monogamy as a normal standard for family laws. Western philosophers believed that monogamous marriage brings fundamental private goods to the married couple and their children as well as the basic goodness of the society. Therefore these philosophers view polygamy as a crime because it promotes inequity, confuses children, and jeopardise the sanctity of marital consent. To the Western philosopher whose way of thinking is impacted by worldly material things, polygamy is a source of punishment because when the man dies, the wives and children in the polygamous home share the estate rather than only a monogamous wife and children inheriting everything. The naturalists view monogamous marriage as the best way to ensure equal dignity and respect between men and women while others believe that monogamous marriage defends traditional family values by rational appeals based on anthropology and evolutionary science. The writer John Witt, Jr classified criticism of polygamy into 4: Biblical, Natural, Harm-based and Symbolic. The first two highlighted the difference between the criticisms relating to polygamy and same-sex marriages while the other two are specific to polygamy. Most interest is the harm-based which most Western philosophers used to criticising polygamy and this continues to date with argument that polygamy is often the cause of harm. Women in polygamous marriages according to the western philosophers suffer from increased levels of sexual and physical abuse against them, lower equality for women, higher discrimination against women, increased rate of female genital mutilations, and increased rate of female sex-trafficking. Monogamous family is therefore considered as a private pillar of public life, the so-called little commonwealth referred to as the first society. It is therefore important that the political systems should encourage relationships that promote public health, safety, and welfare. To the Western philosophers, that relationship is monogamy. These are very interesting arguments because the same Western philosophers who argues against what they perceived to be "Islamic" promoted action (polygamy) supports a man to have one wife and hundreds concubines! That is why the Western society is broke to the point that fixing it would require spiritual interventions based on the cradle of Islam. A chat with a Western lady would reveal one sadness: many women are not getting married to the men they met and loved because the man has a wife. Based on that she becomes a sex machine where the man craving for sex would just call and visit her where they have sex and he leaves after work to his married wife. This is the most evil cruelty and degrading act that some women face. Society cannot run away from the fact that men in monogamous marriages cheat their wives although some men in polygamous marriages also cheat. This idea of promoting the so-called "women to sex" has led to increased number of same sex marriage because the western philosophers have made some women to believe that men are beasts so if she wants to find a caring love, then she should look for that in her fellow woman! Similar argument was put forward regarding men with the belief that women are parasites who depends on the hard work of men so men should look for love from their fellow men! What readers must note is same-sex marriage was fought against by the church although of late some churches have started accepting same-sex marriage as norm while polygamy was sanctioned by the political and legal systems. In Murphy vs. Ramsey (1885), the US Supreme court made the following declaration: *"Certainly no legislation can be supposed more wholesome and necessary in the founding of a free, self-governing commonwealth, fit to take rank as one of the coordinate States of the Union, than that which seeks to establish it on the basis of the idea of the family, as consisting in and springing from the union for life of one man and one woman in the holy estate of matrimony; the sure foundation of all that is stable and noble in our civilization; the best guaranty of that reverent morality which is the source of all beneficent progress in social and political improvement."* A previous law (1882) disqualified polygamists from voting rights, sitting on jurors, and holding public office while in Reynolds vs. United States (1879), the US Supreme court turned aside claims of free exercise of religion lodged by polygamists.

With regards to the status of women, the western society views women to be agent of money making machines with almost all advertising materials that involved women prefer to showcase women in an insulting manner where they must reveal their nakedness before they are paid! In addition, in the West, the so-called "feminization" of human rights continues to draw the anger of some men who in turn subject women to horrific punishment such as rape and even killings. Because the Western system is just interested in the morality of money, women have lost the moral sense so promoting the very act that the human rights groups said they are fighting against: Infanticide! The so-called "western lady" has been programmed to believe that she needs to go out work hard like a donkey in order to contribute to the wellbeing of the family. In order for her to fulfil this, the "western lady" would prefer to have abortion rather given birth to a child! All these are abhorred at in Islam. As outline in his last sermon, the Prophet (SAW) advised Muslims about women:

"O people! Fear Allah concerning women. Verily you have taken them on the security of Allah and have made their persons lawful unto you by the Words of Allah! Verily, you have got certain rights over your women, and your women have certain rights over you. It is rights and, not to commit act of impropriety which, if they do, you have authority to chastise them, yet not severely. If your wives refrain from impropriety and faithful to you, clothe and feed them suitably. "

Can anyone argue with me that this is the best advice ever given on how to treat a woman? The honour bestowed on women by Islam is so great when compared to how Western system advocate for the right of women. What these Western Philosophers do not understand is, in the beautiful religion of Islam, women are held in high esteem and regarded as partners in life to men. Women in Islam, in contrary to what the Western Philosophers narration are not subject of slavery nor regarded as second human beings like the West. It is the West that regards certain people like black and the Palestinians as second global citizens and women are expected to work like donkeys in order to support the family. Islam promotes women to be educated, work moderately for livelihood and be obedient to their husbands and as advice by Muhammad (SAW), no matter their status in the society, it is the responsibility of men to feed and clothe them. In a Facebook message, a friend once argued by asking a question: why should women follow the narrative of the west and keep working to contribute to the wellbeing of the family? In Islam, a woman's responsibility is on her husband but if she doesn't have a husband it falls on her family. The Islamic type of woman is supposed to be queen! Unfortunately the western philosophers and their stooges have removed the honour bestowed on women and made women the most degraded human being of our generation!

THE RELIGION OF KNOWLEDGE

Some non-Muslim always attributes the spread of Islam to the power of the sword while others hold the opinion that because Muslims believe in judgement day, it means Islam does not promote any act that facilitate advancement such as acquiring knowledge. Their arguments is of what use it is that you acquire all material gains yet die to face some sort of judgement. These contemporary scholars do not understand Islam properly. Great non-Islamic scholars such as Ignac Goldziher, Joseph Schacht and Michael Cook were so confused about Islam that they became critiques of the religion while other modern scholar such as Salman Rushdie became so blinded that understanding what Islam is became a problem. Of all the religions, it is only Islam that started with knowledge when the Holy Prophet (SAW) was asked to "read". I won't deal with the scientific proves of the Quran. This would insha Allah be in my forthcoming book "Scientific Verses". The late Dr Kwame Nkrumah of Ghana advised Africans in one of his famous speeches that Africans need to develop their mental ability before thinking of economy advancement. Dr Nkrumah was then highlighting the importance of seeking knowledge which was earlier recommended by the greatest human being to grace this world (SAW). Islam was not spread by sword as is being wrongly disseminated or believed by non-Islamic scholars. In the Holy Quran, Allah (SWT) entreated us that:

> **"There shall be no compulsion in the religion. The right course has become clear from the wrong"** (2: 256).

In this verse, Allah (SWT) was asking Muslims not to enforce the religion on anybody but individuals are recommended to ponder over what the religion stands for then make their choice for the truthfulness of Islam is crystal clear. That is why presently, the fastest growing religion in the world is Islam. Humanity finding itself at the brink where the same acts that set the period of Jahilliya as period of ignorance is now happening before our very eyes. Despite the so-called technological advancement, man is so blinded by power and fame that killings are order of the day. Unlike in the Jahilliya period, now it is not only infanticide but" humanicide" is been perpetuated at an alarming rate. Innocent people are being killed just because the strong want to forcibly take away lands, etc from the defenceless people and the world just watches! With this humanity has started asking the morality of our living and through that have started studying Islam to have proper understanding of the religion that has been able to withstand all the propaganda of the Western system including philosophy and political systems. After studying Islam, they deduce the perfectness of the call (of Islam) and they realises that these Western system had lied and betrayed them!

Islam as a peaceful was not propagated by the power of sword as promulgated by the bias scholars. The historian, Thomas Carlyle said in his book titled 'Heroes and Hero worship' while referring to the misconception that the sword was used in spreading Islam wrote: *'the sword indeed, but where will you get the sword? Every opinion, at its starting is precisely in a minority of one; in one man's head alone. There it dwells as yet. One man alone of the whole world believes it, there is one man against all men. That he takes sword and tries to propagate with that will do little to him. You must get your sword! On the whole, a thing will propagate itself as it can."*

Another historian, De Lacy O'Leary also wrote: *"History makes it clear however, that the legend of fanatical Muslims sweeping through the world and forcing Islam at the point of the sword upon conquered races is one of the most fantastically absurd myths that historians have ever repeated."* And sadly enough they keep repeating that myth!

When the religion was revealed through Archangel Jibril (AS), it was only to the Holy Prophet (SAW). When he (SWA) went home, he lied on bed afraid about the encounter he (SAW) had with an angel. His beloved wife, Nana Khadijah (May Allah be pleased with her) covered him with a mantle then the verse:

"O you wrapped up (in the mantle)! Arise and warn, and your Lord do you magnify, and your garments do purify, and uncleanness do shun" (74: 1-5).

This verse has one spiritual message to humanity: when you want something, you need to get up and work hard for it. If not the sword, what led to Islam spreading? We can start our fact presentation with the recommendation by Allah (SWT) when He (SWT) advised us:

"Invite to the way of your Lord with wisdom and good instruction, and argue with them in a way that is best" (16:125).

Two terms are used here which are of importance: "wisdom" and "good instruction". What is wisdom? There are many meanings of wisdom but one that fits this narrative is "intelligence". This means the first suggestion by Allah (SWT) to His (SWT) creators is to use knowledge to debate with people about Islam. One does not have to use force or any weapons to fight people on the basis of convincing them to convert to Islam. The use of intelligence and good instruction was best exhibited when some companions migrated to the present day Ethiopia and Eritrea after severe prosecution by the people of Mecca. The king at that time was named An-Nagashi who was referred to as just king by the Prophet (SAW). Later the leaders of Quraysh sent emissary to convince the just king who was a Christian to bring them (the Muslims) back. During the debate between the Muslim and the Quraysh emissary, the Muslims used wisdom and good character to defend the religion (Islam). After listening to both parties, the king drew a line and proclaimed *"the difference between the message of Mohammad (SAW) and Christianity is the difference between this thin line."* He then told the Muslims that they can live in peace in Ethiopia and he would protect them as much as he would protect the Christian citizen of his realm. The simple question to ask here is: Would the king have accepted the narration of the Muslims if they had lacked wisdom and bad character?

No! That was the best of Islam on display on that historical moment when the entire lives and faith of these migrants was at stake! Their way of living was so convincing that the king later converted to Islam.

Before we analyse the wars the Prophet (SAW) in order to debunk the false myth that Islam was spread by the power of sword, we should take a look at the conquest of Mecca. The conquest of Mecca took place on the 20th day of Ramadan in the year 8 AH. What can we learn from this conquest? Muslims had experienced horrific persecution in Mecca which resulted in Muslims migrating to Medina. Over the next few years, Muslims and the Quraysh of Mecca engaged in series of battles. The battles came to a temporary halt when the Prophet (SAW) and the people of Quraysh signed a peace treaty, after the Muslims were denied the right to enter Mecca for religious duty. The treaty was agreed to last for 10 years. One of the terms of the treaty was any tribe outside Mecca or Medina was allowed to choose to either align to Muslims or the Quraysh. However, if any of these tribes had altercations, neither the Muslims nor the Quraysh could support their allies against the other's allies. A tribe called Banu Khuza'ah aligned themselves with Muslims and accepted Islam, whilst Banu Bakr aligned with Quraysh. Within some few years, the Quraysh not only violated the treaty by supported Banu Bakr to fight Banu Khuza'ah and also participated in killing some Muslims among them; excluding one person who fled and sought refuge in the sacred Ka'bah. With this violation of the House of Allah (SWT), the treaty was officially broken. As explained by Aisha (RA), she had never seen the Holy Prophet (SAW) angrier than when he (SAW) was told of the violation of the treaty. With the violation, one consequence was final: the conquest of Mecca.

After the conquest, the Holy Prophet (SAW) addressed the people and asked them what he should he do with them? They answered: *'You are our noble brother, son of our noble brother! We expect nothing but good news from you.'*

Let us analyse this confrontation. If it was either you or me, what would we do? We have seen nations taken decision to collectively punish people because of the action of few people. A typical example is the reaction of Israel against the innocent people of Gaza) where more than 23,000 innocent people (as the time of writing this book) have been killed just because a crazy war criminal thinks he has the right to kill people.

But on that day, he (SAW) told them:

'I say to you as Yusuf (Joseph) said to his brothers, "No blame upon you today. Allah has forgiven you, for He is the Most Merciful of the merciful."

In another narration he told them: *'Go, you are free.'*

Is this not beautiful? Those who accuse the Prophet (SAW) that he (SAW) was just interested in power would argue with us that he (SAW) intentionally forgave them in order to acquire power. Strange! The man who at the very beginning was assured power that has never been seen and wealth beyond the imagination of humans by the Quraysh but told them:

'I would fight and never rest till the words of Allah reigns'

He never said till I acquire power! He (SWT) was sent as a mercy to humanity.

After the conquest of Mecca, Allah (SWT) told us in the Holy Quran:

"When the victory of Allah has come and the conquest (Mecca), and you see the people entering into the religion of Allah in multitudes, then exalt (Him) with praise of your Lord and ask forgiveness of Him. Indeed, He is ever accepting of repentance" (110:1-3)"

He (SAW) as described by Nana Aisha (RA) was the "walking Quran" so he (SAW) forgave them because Allah (SWT) forgave them. He (SAW) never took religious decision on his (SAW) own. He (SAW) only conveyed what Allah (SWT) commanded him (SAW) to do. This book cannot describe in details the forgiving traits of the Holy Prophet (SAW) but this brief analysis should finally close the chapter of those who disseminate the false myth that Islam was spread by the power of the sword. The man Muhammad (SAW) was so great that Michael Hart named him (SAW) the greatest man to ever live both in the religious and secular realms! When he (Hart) was asked why did he named Muhammad (SAW) the greatest man, he (Hart) answered: *" My choice of Muhammad to lead the list of the world's most influential persons may surprise some readers and may be questioned by others, but he was the only man in history who was supremely successful on both the religious and secular level."* In his comment about the Prophet (SAW), the great Indian leader and scholar Mahatma Ghandi said: *"From my reading I received the impression that the Prophet was a seeker of Truth. He was God-fearing. In this I know I am not telling you anything new. I am only describing to you how I was impressed by his life. He suffered endless persecution. He was brave and feared no man but God alone. He did what he considered to be right in scorn of consequences. He was never found to say one thing and do another. He acted as he felt. If there was a change in his opinion, the next day he responded to the change without counting the cost and regardless of popular censure or opposition. The Prophet was a Fakir. He renounced everything. He could have commanded wealth if he had so desired."* Gandhi was right for the man Muhammad (SAW) was never a seeker of wealth. He was always seeking and fighting for the Truth (God). For all his status, sometimes he went for loans from Jews because there was no money in the house to even cook food! But this was a man whose companions could lay their lives for! Hart and Gandhi were not the only non-Muslims to give none bias testimonies about the Prophet (SAW). Edward Gibbon who was English historian and Member of Parliament wrote: *"The good sense of Muhammad despised the pomp of royalty. The Apostle of God submitted to the menial offices of the family; he kindled the fire; swept the floor; milked the ewes; and mended with his own hands his shoes and garments. Disdaining the penance and merit of a hermit, he observed without effort of vanity the abstemious diet of an Arab."*

Thomas Carlyle, a Scottish philosopher, historian, and writer wrote: *"It is a great shame for anyone to listen to the accusation that Islam is a lie and that Muhammad was a fabricator and a deceiver. We saw that he remained steadfast upon his principles, with firm determination; kind and generous, compassionate, pious, virtuous, with real manhood, hardworking and sincere. Besides all these qualities, he was lenient with others, tolerant, kind, cheerful and praiseworthy and perhaps he would joke and tease his companions. He was just, truthful, smart, pure, magnanimous and present-minded ..."*

"Muhammad was a shining example to his people. His character was pure and stainless. His house, his dress, his food – they were characterized by a rare simplicity. So unpretentious was he that he would receive from his companions no special mark of reverence, nor would he accepts any service

from his slave which he could do for himself. He was accessible to all and at all times. He visited the sick and was full of sympathy for all. Unlimited was his benevolence and generosity as also was his anxious care for the welfare of the community." Reverend Bosworth Smith, an American bishop and a scholar wrote: *"Head of the State as well as the Church, he was Caesar and Pope in one; but he was Pope without the Pope's pretensions, Caesar without the legions of Caesar: without a standing army, without a bodyguard, without a palace, without fixed revenue. If ever any man had the right to say that he ruled by the right divine, it was Mohammed, for he had all the power without its instruments and without its supports. He cared not for all the dressings of power. The simplicity of his private life was in keeping with his public life."* Stanley Edward Lane-Poole, a British orientalist and archaeologist: *"He was the most faithful protector of those he protected, the sweetest and most agreeable in conversation. Those who saw him were suddenly filled with reverence; those who came near him loved him; they who described him would say, "I have never seen his like either before or after." He was of great taciturnity, but when he spoke it was with emphasis and deliberation, and no one could forget what he said ..."*

The great French statesman, write, and poet, Alphonse de Lamartine: *"If greatness of purpose, smallness of means, and astonishing results are the three criteria of a human genius, who could dare compare any great man in history with Muhammad? The most famous men created arms, laws, and empires only. They founded, if anything at all, no more than material powers which often crumbled away before their eyes. This man moved not only armies, legislations, empires, peoples, dynasties, but millions of men in one-third of the then inhabited world; and more than that, he moved the altars, the gods, the religions, the ideas, the beliefs and the souls ... As regards all standards by which human greatness may be measured, we may well ask, is there any man greater than he?"*

Annie Besant who was a British rights' activist, socialist, and orator: *"It is impossible for anyone who studies the life and character of the great Prophet of Arabia, who knows how he taught and how he lived, to feel anything but reverence for that mighty Prophet, one of the great messengers of the Supreme. And although in what I put to you I shall say many things which may be familiar to many, yet I myself feel whenever I re-read them, a new way of admiration, a new sense of reverence for that mighty Arabian teacher."*

Christiaan Snouck Hurgronje, a Dutch scholar and government advisor: *"The league of nations founded by the prophet of Islam put the principle of international unity and human brotherhood on such universal foundations as to show candle to other nations … The world has not hesitated to raise to divinity individuals whose lives and missions have been lost in legend. Historically speaking, none of these legends achieved even a fraction of what Muhammad accomplished. And all his striving was for the sole purpose of uniting mankind for the worship of One God on the codes of moral excellence. Muhammad or his followers never at any time claimed that he was a Son of God or the God-incarnate or a man with divinity – but he always was and is even today considered as only a Messenger chosen by God."* William Montgomery Watt, a Scottish historian, orientalist, and Anglican priest: *"His readiness to undergo persecutions for his beliefs, the high moral character of the men who believed in him and looked up to him as leader, and the greatness of his ultimate achievement – all argue his fundamental integrity. To suppose Muhammad an impostor raises more problems than it solves. Moreover, none of the great figures of history is so poorly appreciated in the West as Muhammad."* One of the greatest Western philosophers provided a novel solution to the global problems confronting us. George Bernard Shaw who was Irish playwright, critic and political activist in his sincere comment about Muhammad (SAW) wrote: *"The world is in dire need of a man with the mind of Muhammad; religious people in the Middle-Ages, due to their ignorance and prejudice, had pictured him in a very dark way as they used to consider him the enemy of Christianity. But after looking into the story of this man I found it to be an amazing and a miraculous one and I came to the conclusion that he was never an enemy of Christianity, and must be called instead the savoir of humanity. In my opinion, if he was to be given control over the world today, he would solve our problems and secure the peace and happiness which the world is longing for."*

How I wished Bernard Shaw was alive for me to visit and thank him for this excellent suggestion! In this period of chaos when we don't know the direction the world is taking, Bernard recommended we need a person with the mindset of Muhammad (SAW). In summary what Bernard Shaw was advising the world is we now need another Muhammad who can stand for truth and be a means to our problems? William Montgomery Watt made a very interesting observation when he suggested that the West never appreciated Muhammad (SAW) for the moral, political, economy, and religious tolerance he (SAW) promoted. These rare traits were the reason he (SAW) was able to conquer the hearts of humanity that many years after his (SAW) death, many people are still cherishing him (SAW) and ready to lay their lives for him (SAW). But why does the West not appreciate him? The answer is simple: Those in authorities hide any positive trait of this great man (SAW) but instead twist the facts and rather concentrate on propagating false information about him (SAW) through their media. I remember encounter with this good Christian friend who held the believer: *Why should I a scholar believe in Muhammad?* I was really shocked because she was also a scholar. I then asked her why she thought I should not believe in him. She answer: *"He (SAW) brought darkness to the world by promoting polygamy and killed people to spread his believe."* That is how the Western media and political system twist the mind of their ordinary people because they are afraid that when they come to know who Muhammad stands for, they would as the Quran predicted run to the religion of Muhammad (SAW) for their salvations. Those who want to learn about Islam and Prophet Muhammad (SAW) should learn with open mind. One Christian friend once advised me: *"Read the Bible with open mind and you would find the truth."* Six months after his recommendation, I went back to him and told him: *"My dear friend, I have read the Bible inside out with open mind and I found that Muhammad (SAW) and Islam is where I belong." Can you do the same with the Quran?"* Later, he came to me and amazingly said: *"My brother, Islam is the right religion but I fear that if I accept the religion I will have problems with my family!"* Today my friend is a renowned Christian preacher and anytime I meet him I asked him: *"Do you still believe in Muhammad (SAW) and Quran?"* Always his answer is 'yes' but for reasons best known to him, he refuses to be a Muslim.

Having debunked the falsified notion the West holds about Muhammad (SAW) let's turn our attention to why I refer Islam as the religion of knowledge? To Plato, the father of Western philosophy made this interesting description about knowledge and wisdom: *"If a man neglects education, he walks lame to the end". A library of wisdom is more precious than all wealth, and all things that are desirable cannot be compared to it. Whoever therefore claims to be zealous of truth, of happiness, of wisdom or knowledge must become a lover of books. And what, Socrates, is the food of the* soul? Surely, I said, knowledge is the food of the soul. Writing is the geometry of the soul. A good decision is based on knowledge and not on numbers. Books give a soul to the universe, wings to the mind, flight to the imagination, and life to everything. Ideas are the source of all things"

From these, Plato is referring to knowledge as the soul and emancipator of human being. This means any system that promotes knowledge is also promoting human being to be a good person. I must however add there are some who seek knowledge then use it in attempting to destroy humanity as rightly advised by Plato: *"knowledge becomes evils if the aim be not virtuous"*. Based on this, the seeker of knowledge should be guided by the principle of Light (God). Knowledge is the weapon that can be used to change all things. The South African leader Nelson Mandela once said: *"Education (knowledge) is the most powerful weapon which you can use to change the world."*

The first verse revealed to the Muhammad (SAW) was Surah Al-Alaq. When Muhammad (SAW) encountered Angel Jibril (AS), the angel asked Muhammad (SAW) to read but because he was unlettered, he (SAW) told the angel he couldn't read. After the angel had repeated the same words, Muhammad (SAW) asked him what he should read then advice:

> **"Read in the name of your Lord who created, created man from clots of congealed blood. Read! Your Lord is the Most Bountiful One, who taught by the pen, taught man what he did not know. Indeed, man transgresses in thinking himself self-sufficient. Verily to your Lord is the return. Have you seen the man who forbids a servant when he prays? Have you seen if he follows the right guidance or enjoins piety? Think: if he denies the truth and give no heed, does he not know that Allah observes all things? Let him desist, or We will drag him by the forelock, his lying, sinful forelock. Then let him call his helpmates. We, in Our turn, will call the angels of punishment. No, never obey him? Prostrate yourself and come nearer (96)**

Three words are of essence: "Read" "Taught" and "transgresses". These words point to the direction that one needs when seeking knowledge: one must turn the books as friends and should look for a teacher to impart knowledge in him but do not think after acquiring the knowledge you would transgress and start thinking that you are above God therefore self-sufficient and do not require God again. Knowledge should rather make it seeker humble! That is why Allah (SWT) says in the Holy Quran

> **"We bestowed wisdom on Luqman (saying): 'Give thanks to Allah. He that gives thanks to Him has much to gain, but if any is ungrateful, Allah is Self-sufficient and Glorious"** (31:12).

This means when one acquires knowledge (wisdom), it should not give one false sense of self-sufficient for Self-sufficient is an attribute for Allah only. The Quran consist of verses that promotes and advices human beings to seek for knowledge. My favourite verse is:

> **"Is he who supplicates in the watches of the night, prostrating and standing, apprehensive of the Hereafter and expecting the mercy of his Lord ...? Say, 'Are those who know equal to those who do not know?' Only those who possess intellect take admonition".** (39:9).

In this verse, Allah is telling us that one cannot compare those who possess knowledge to those who do not.

> **"There is no god but He: that is the witness of Allah, His angels, and those who endued with knowledge, standing firm on justice. There is no god but He the Exalted in Power, the Wise"** (3:18).

In this holy verse, Allah starts with Himself then ranks angels next to Him than men of knowledge. This is an honour, good value, and superiority that Allah associates to men of knowledge.

In another verse, Allah says:

"It is those who endued with knowledge from amongst Allah's servants that fear Allah most" (35:28).

Here, Allah is telling us (humanity) that those who fear Him most are men of knowledge. I must however, add that history has taught us stories of individuals who are well educated but they became nemesis to humanity. They caused so much pain to humanity that mentioning their names brings memories of death to mankind!

In another verse, Allah said:

"But even, it (the Quran) is of evidently clear signs in the breasts of those endued with knowledge" (29:49).

In another verse, Allah said:

"He created man, and taught him speech (and intelligence)" (55:3-4).

Allah said further:

"We should then relate to them (the narrations) with knowledge" (7:52)

In these verses above, Allah (SWT) was reminding humanity the blessings He (SWT) has bestowed on humanity. It shows that Allah (SWT) wants mankind to engage in seeking for knowledge.

Now let's turn to the man Muhammad (SAW) and analyse his stance on knowledge.

His famous recommendation on knowledge is: *"Seeking for knowledge is an obligation upon every Muslim."*

In this recommendation, the Holy Prophet (SAW) advised Muslim to seek for knowledge and made it mandatory for Muslims to seek for knowledge.

In another recommendation, he (SAW) said:

"Seek after knowledge even though it is to (take you as far as to) China."

Why did he (SAW) mention China? First, because the distance between Mecca and China at that time was so far as they used horse and camels. Therefore travelling to China was not only extremely difficult but also dangerous. Second, China was and remains a communist country which in the past does not believe in God. So for the prophet (SAW) to advise us (Muslim) to travel as far as China outlines how the religion of Allah regards knowledge. The Prophet (SAW) had this wonderful advice to mankind: *"No doubt, the learned men are the heirs of Prophet (as far as knowledge is concerned)."*

To name people of knowledge as heirs to the Prophets is a huge call as it is known that the Prophets are of higher superiority so for the Prophet (SAW) give them (seekers of knowledge) such accolade means men of knowledge are held in high esteem by the Prophet (SAW) and the religion.

How would you take the death of an entire tribe? It is a known fact that even if one should lose a bread winner, the family is so devastated but the Prophet (SAW) who had always regarded knowledge as the foundation of the religion said: *"No doubt the wholesale death of (all members of a) tribe is much easier than the death of a man endued with knowledge."*

Allah stands for light and in His encounter with Abraham (AS), He (SWT), Muhammad (SAW) narrated that Allah (SWT) told Abraham (AS) said:

"O Abraham! I'm full of knowledge, and I love such (of men) as endued with knowledge".

To continue teaching the importance of knowledge, Muhammad (SAW) had this: *"If a day comes upon me, on which I've not increased in knowledge which brings me closer to Allah Almighty, let not me be blessed in the sunrise of that day."*

Although Muhammad (SAW) mentioned closer to Allah, he (SAW) was advising us that mankind need to acquire knowledge to enable him get closer to the Light (Allah).

In another advise that put seeks of knowledge high, Muhammad (SAW) said: *"On the day of Judgement, there will be three types of intercessors: the Prophets then learned men, and then the martyrs."*

O, the men of knowledge are held in high esteem by the man who came as mercy to humanity (SAW). The men of knowledge are place just after the Prophets for intercession on the day of reckon!

Still discussing about the day of Judgement, Muhammad (SAW) said: *"On the day of Judgement, Allah Almighty will raise the worshipping servant and then He will raise the learned men, and say "O assembly of learned men! I have not provided you with My knowledge by because I have full recognition of you; and I've never given you My knowledge in order to punish you; go I've forgiven you."*

This is a wonderful rank for people of knowledge. Those who are blessed with knowledge should try and use their blessing (knowledge) to help mankind.

The companions saw Muhammad (SAW) physically and after synthesising his (SAW) love for knowledge also developed positive ideology on knowledge.

Ali Ibn Talib (AS) said: *"Let the men of knowledge be proud of being the guides for anyone who seeks the right guidance. Everyone is estimated by what he is able to do perfectly, since the ignorant are always the traditional enemies of the learned men. So acquire knowledge therewith you could live lasting since the people will die, but the men of knowledge will live forever."*

Abu Al-Aswad (AS) also added: *"Nothing is clearer than knowledge: it is true that the king rile over the people m the learned men rule over the kings."* Ash-Shafi (RA) said: *"To seek knowledge is much better than to perform voluntary services"* Ibn Abu Al-Malik also who said: *"I was with Malik Ibn Anas reciting portion of knowledge to him when the due time of Zuhur prayer came upon them, thereupon I gathered the books in order to offer prayer. On that he said: "O man! By no means is that prayer to which you've stood to offer better than that state of studying knowledge in which you were, on the condition that the intention should be right."*

Some people have been accusing Muslims of promoting jihad, a holy war waged on the behalf of Islam as a religious duty. But there is one action that is equal to jihad as explained by Abu Ad-Darda: *"He, who thinks that going early in the morning with the intention to acquire knowledge is not Jihad, is indeed lacking in both his though and mind,."*

Finally Fath Al-Nawal (AS) added: *"Is it not if food and drink are forbidden to a sick person, he will die?"* When they answered yes, he then added: *"So is the case of mind: if knowledge and wisdom are forbidden to it for three days, it will die."* Fath (AS) made the right assertion. The human body needs food to nourish the body. Similarly, the mind is nourished by knowledge and wisdom. This means if the mind is derived of knowledge and wisdom, the mind dies.

Umar ibn Khattab (AS) also said: *"O people, I advise you to stick to knowledge for Allah Almighty has a garment which He loves, and whoever seeks for any branch knowledge, he will be dressed by Allah Almighty in this garment and if he commits a sin, he will be asked to turn in repentance thrice, in order not to deprive him of that garment; even though he insists on committing that sin and dies."*

Knowledge is therefore of utmost importance in Islam as supported by Luqman (AS) to his son: *"O my son! Sit with the learned men, and compete with them in (learning), for Allah Almighty gives life to minds with the help of the light of wisdom, in the same was as He gives life to earth with the help of the rain which comes down from the sky."*

Ali Ibn Talib, the great man of knowledge (AS) said: *"No doubt, the learned one is much better than the fasting person, who stands at night for supererogatory prayers, and practice Jihad; if a learned man dies, his death causes a gap to happen in Islam, which could not be filled up but by a successor to him."*

In another sermon, he (AS) said: *"Let the men of knowledge be proud of being the guides for anyone who seeks the right guidance. Everyone is estimated by what he is able to do perfectly, since the ignorant are always traditional enemies of the learned men. So, acquire knowledge therewith you could live lastingly since people will die, but the men of knowledge will live forever."*

In the previous sermon, Ali Ibn Talib compared learning to some extremely significant act in Islam: fasting, supererogatory prayers in the night, and jihad and he (AS) concluded that learning is better than these acts. In the second sermon, Ali Ibn Talib (AS) advised that we should seek for knowledge so that one' name will live forever because any education material one left behind after death would be read by generation upon generation.

How do we substantiate the argument that Islam is a religion of knowledge? We can give the answer by critically evaluating the five pillars of Islam which are: to bear testimony there is no god worth worship than Allah, performing prayers, paying zakat, fasting in the month of Ramadan, and going to hajj if you can. All these principles require one to possess knowledge so that you are able to perform them to a satisfactory level. When a child attains the age of puberty, the first obligation on him is to learn and understand the meaning of 'there is no god worth worship than Allah'. He requires knowledge for him to understand this principle. From the early phase of life, man is made to understand that you are guided by certain principle and that principle is dependent on you understanding the statement of affirmation (Kalimatu Shahada). One does not have to start researching but the obligation upon him is to understand and learn the meaning of this principle. After fulfilling the first principle, man is expected as an obligation to fulfil the obligation of praying. First, he is required to have knowledge on how to perform ablution and purification baths. After, he learns and understands how to perform prayers. He must learn how to stand in the right manner, perform the right bowing and prostration. If he forgets or add something, how to correct his prayers if he makes a mistake. He must know the compulsory and non-compulsory aspect of prayers. He must learn how to recite the opening chapter and any other chapters to enable him perform his prayers well. The necessity of acquiring knowledge to perform all these is essential for this obligation.

When he reached the age allowed to perform fasting, he is expected to learn and understand what are required of him; such as how to make intention for fasting, what breaks the fasting, why he has to refrain from eating and sexual activities during the period. During fasting, he is required to be calm and should refrain from fighting as recommended by Muhammad (SAW). He should understand that as soon as the fasting begins, he is expected to follow the month till the new moon is seen.

When he attains adulthood and if capable, he has to give zakat (obligatory charity) from his earning. He needs to learn and understand why this is obligatory on man. He has to understand who should be giving the zakat and how to calculate the zakat (although this is not mandatory).

When he is capable, he should go for Hajj. It is necessary for him to learn all the obligations associated with Hajj including the ceremonies and duties. He should have the knowledge on what should not be performed during Hajj such as unnecessary talking; avoid certain things such as sex with legitimate partner, or killing. He should understand that he must not take part in these and other prohibited activities. These five pillars require a Muslim to acquire knowledge and by making this obligatory, it means acquiring the knowledge to perform them is also obligatory.

After these obligatory duties, a Muslim is guided by the principle of goodness and fighting evilness as Allah recommended in the Quran that Satan is our enemy so we should become his enemy. To develop this principle of goodness, man has to always learn and understand how to live with his neighbours, how to carry business, how to deal with non-Muslims, etc. All these are based on the principle of learning and understanding which required knowledge. When man goes into marriage, he must learn how to perform his duties within marriage and if he decides to engage in polygamous marriage, he must always learn and understand how he should be just to his wives and children. During his business activities, he must learn and understand that cheating is prohibited and those who engage in business that involves measurement should understand and learn the principle of measurement. When engaged in industries such as farming, politics, and science, a Muslim must know what is right and what is wrong. Understanding and learning is a prerequisite for Muslim to perform his daily activities. When he is blessed with children, a Muslim must know and learn how to take care of his children. In the society he lives, a Muslim is expected to be a good ambassador of Islam so he must learn and understand the Islamic recommendation on living in harmony with people in his community to the extent that Muhammad (SAW) once remarked

> *"Angel Jibril (AS) advised me continuously to take care of the neighbour till I thought Allah is to make him (neighbour) an inheritor".*

When a Muslim's parent grows old, he must learn and understand how he should take care of them. Finally, when there is death, a Muslim must have an understanding on how to pray for the deceased and how to bury the dead. From these discussions, we can deduce that a Muslim is expected to start learning till he dies. That is why Muhammad (SAW) said:

> *"Seeking knowledge is compulsory on Muslims."*

This means acquiring knowledge is the fulcrum of our religion thereby making Islam the religion of knowledge. In this era when humanity is focused on worldly affairs that a man is judged by the number of properties or funds in his bank account. This has resulted in humanity becoming too stress with mass and ritual killings reported around the world on daily basis. If humanity should listen to the advice of Muhammad (SAW) and acquire good knowledge, the chaos that the world finds itself would surely come to an end. In his remark, William Shakespeare said: 'What *a terrible era in which idiots govern the blind.' We can regenerate our eyes by acquiring knowledge!*

In conclusion, the Prophet (SAW) in emphasising the importance of seeking for knowledge said:

> *"No doubt, the learned are the heirs of Prophets (as far as knowledge is concerned)."*

For Muhammad (SAW) to raised the seekers of knowledge to the rank of Prophets, the highest ranked individuals before Allah shows the significant of knowledge to man.

We must therefore be seekers of knowledge for Jesus (AS) advised us: *"He, who learns, act (upon what he learns) and has knowledge (of what he does) will be called Great one among the assemble of angels of the heavens."*

ZAKAT-THE BEST FORM OF DONATION FOR ENDING POVERTY

❈

Zakat is an Islamic obligation where an individual donates a certain portion of his/her wealth each year for charitable purposes. It is one of the main principles of Islam. The word zakat is derived from the word "Zakd" which means "it grew". The second derivation carries a sense of purification such as "Qad aflaha man zakkaha" meaning "he is indeed successful who purified himself". When one evaluates these words, one can draw a conclusion to their significance for when man spends his wealth for the sake of Allah, Allah purifies his heart from the love of material wealth. When man spends his wealth as humble gift before His Lord, he is affirming that nothing is dearer to him in life than the love of Allah and that he is fully prepared to sacrifice everything for the sake of Allah. Man, by nature would protect his wealth with every blood in his vein but to be prepared to give part of his wealth as zakat for the sake of Allah is a unique form of worship. In the Holy Quran, zakat is mentioned 82 times and closely associated with prayers (Salat). The 2nd and 3rd pillars of Islam are establishing prayers and giving zakat, respectively. From this we can argue that zakat has religious and spiritual aspect while it economic aspect cannot be denied for zakat is one of the best mechanisms of improving the economic conditions of the have-nots. Since I am not an expert in how to calculate zakat, I won't be discussing the how and when should zakat be paid. For these, there are many experts' views which readers can consult.

Allah says in the surah Al-Muzzammil (73:20)

> **"Yet you shall duly establish the prayer. And you shall give the Zakat, and therewith lend Allah a most goodly loan. For whatever good you advance for your souls, you shall find its reward with God in the Hereafter; yet it shall be far better and much greater in reward."**

In surah Al-Mujadilah (58:13), Allah says:

> **"Then steadfastly continue to duly establish prayer. And give the Zakat**

While in Surah Fussilat (41:7), He (SWT) says:

> **"For woe to those who associate gods with God, those who do not give the Zakat, those who are disbelievers in the Hereafter."**

In Surah Tawbah (9:60), Allah (SWT) says with regards to how zakat should be distributed:

> **"Indeed, prescribed charitable offerings are only to be given to the poor and the indigent, and those who work on administering it, and those whose hearts are to be reconciled, and to free those in bondage, and to the debt-ridden, and for the cause of Allah, and to the wayfarer/ This is an obligation from Allah. And Allah is all-knowing, all-wise."**

The Holy Prophet (SAW) had these to say about zakat as narrated by Abu Hurairah: *"(On the Day of Resurrection) camels will come to their owner in the best state of health they have ever had (in the world), and if he had not paid their Zakat (in the world) then they would tread him with their feet; and similarly, sheep will come to their owner in the best state of health they have ever had in the world, and if he had not paid their Zakat, then they would tread him with their hooves and would butt him with their horns."* The

Prophet added, *"One of their rights is that they should be milked while water is kept in front of them."*

The Prophet added: *"I do not want anyone of you to come to me on the Day of Resurrection, carrying over his neck a sheep that will be bleating. Such a person will (then) say, 'O Muhammad! (Please intercede for me,) I will say to him. 'I can't help you, for I conveyed Allah's Message to you.' Similarly, I do not want anyone of you to come to me carrying over his neck a camel that will be grunting. Such a person (then) will say "O Muhammad! (Please intercede for me)." I will say to him, "I can't help you for I conveyed Allah's message to you."*

In another Narration, Al-Ahnaf bin Qais recounted that the Prophet (SAW) said:*"While I was sitting with some people from Quraish, a man with very rough hair, clothes, and appearance came and stood in front of us, greeted us and said, "Inform those who hoard wealth, that a stone will be heated in the Hell-fire and will be put on the nipples of their breasts till it comes out from the bones of their shoulders and then put on the bones of their shoulders till it comes through the nipples of their breasts the stone will be moving and hitting." After saying that, the person retreated and sat by the side of the pillar, I followed him and sat beside him, and I did not know who he was. I said to him, "I think the people disliked what you had said." He said, "These people do not understand anything, although my friend told me." I asked, "Who is your friend?" He said, "The Prophet said (to me), 'O Abu Dhar! Do you see the mountain of Uhud?' And on that I (Abu Dhar) started looking towards the sun to judge how much remained of the day as I thought that Allah's Apostle wanted to send me to do something for him and I said, 'Yes!' He said, 'I do not love to have gold equal to the mountain of Uhud unless I spend it all (in Allah's cause) except three Dinars (pounds). These people do not understand and collect worldly wealth. No, by Allah, Neither I ask them for worldly benefits nor am I in need of their religious advice till I meet Allah, The Honourable, The Majestic."*

From this verse, there are eight prospective beneficiaries of zakat:

- Poor
- Needy
- Employee of zakat funds
- Those whose heart as been reconsidered
- Freeing slaves
- Debt settlement

- The course of Allah
- The way Fearer

Zakat has spiritual, moral, social, and economic benefits.
For spiritual aspect of zakat, these include:

- Purification of the soul from avarice and greed
- Closeness to Allah as paying zakat is a form of obedient for an order from Allah
- It purifies wealth and results in wealth growing Allah says in Surah Tawba: **"Take from their wealth ˹O Prophet˺ charity to purify and bless them and pray for them—surely your prayer is a source of comfort for them. And Allah is All-Hearing, All-Knowing."**
- Allah's reward is obtained as promised by Allah: **"Who is he that will lend to Allah a goodly loan, then (Allah) will increase it manifold to his credit (in repaying), and he will have (besides) a good reward (i.e. Paradise)." (Surah Al Hadid: 11).**

Social and Economic aspect of zakat

- Helping the poor
- Provision of the needs, of the poor, and the needy
- Redistribution of the wealth in society because the wealth taken from the rich is proportionate to their wealth and given to the poor
- Promote serving and discouragement of concentrating wealth in the hands of the rich
- Helping the course Allah through establishment of religious projects

Moral aspects of zakat:

- Payment of zakat is an indication of obeying Allah
- The payer of zakat would be free of guilt, conscious of seeing the poor for he has made provision for their welfare
- The poor will give good wishes for the rich who through the payment of zakat shows concern of their plight
- The payer of zakat is confident that Allah will bless his/her wealth

The question to be asked is why with this noble social system Muslims are among the poorest people in the world although Islam is the only religion that places emphasis on charity? Some have argued that the system of coordinating such system is primitive in Islam unlike in the Christendom where their charities are well managed through several NGOs and other financial organizations that are established to implement their charities missions unlike within the Muslims communities were systematic processes have not being established for distributions of charities. The sad aspect is Muslims give out more charities than any community in the world yet majority of the poorest individuals are found within the Muslims communities. One just needs to travel to some Muslims communities where poverty is the main cause of social unrest. Muslims gives charities without thinking of getting anything in return because to Muslims by fulfilling our charities duties means we are obeying Allah, our Creator. The answer to the early question is simple: We do not implement the zakat in the proper and prescribed manner. The rich now prefer to give zakat to their friends instead of giving it out to those who really deserve it. In addition, the rich prefers to distribute zakat in such a manner that the receiver of zakat spend it and wait for the next zakat period. It is like a cycle. While Islam has prescribed a perfect social system, Muslims are disoriented and disorganized when implementing one of the pillars of the religion. Unlike prayers and period of Ramadan where there are coordination; with zakat, Muslims address this important pillar individually without any good coordination or institutions, although lately some communities are working hard to coordinate this system. The Holy Quran has emphasised on the social responsibility of a rich Muslims and unlike other religions, Islam is the only religion that places importance of rich Muslims spending his/her money and wealth to assist poor family members and even the extended families. This kind of assistance is a religious duty on every rich Muslims. Beyond this, the rich Muslim should also be helpful to all humanity, including non-Muslims. However, neither the Muslims countries nor communities have developed system that collect and distribute zakat and other Islamic charities. That is the main reason why we see widespread poverty in Muslims countries and communities. The compelling fact is most rich Muslims donates their wealth since it is a religious duty, yet all the funds are not professionally and properly distributed among the poor within Muslims countries and communities. The amount of wealth that rich Muslims distribute among poor Muslims around the world are far bigger than the wealth been given to the poor by the Western rich people. The difference is the Westerners have institutionalised the way they collect and distribute their charities. No religious community is blessed and gifted with a divine social system like Islam which should have enable Muslims to regulate our economic life, yet we are busy fighting over ideological differences thereby failing to develop financial institutions, companies, and banking systems of our own. A fraction of the world's population comprising some greedy capitalistic world leaders and elite companies who control about 90% of the global wealth while billions of people in poor countries suffer from economic hardship. It is modern civilization that has taken humanity into this sad status quo where geopolitical greed and national interests are made priorities than the collective interest of humanity.

The UN Sustainable Goals (SDG) goal 1 states: End poverty in all its form everywhere by 2030. Extreme poverty is defined as "surviving on less than $2.15 per person per day as of 2017 purchasing power parity. If the definition of poverty in 2017 is $2.15, sadly decades after, we have witnessed remarkable decline and now being able to spend $2.15 should not be regarded as poverty. Post-COVID era, people are now living in extreme poverty with almost 90 million living in extreme poverty people when previous predictions are taking into consideration. Before the pandemic, the momentum towards reduction in people living in extreme poverty was slowing down. By the end of 2022, it was suggested approximately 8.4% of the global population (i.e. about 670 million) were living in extreme poverty. If this trend should continue, then by 2030 when SGD goal of ending poverty reaches, instead of reduction, there would be around 575 million people living in extreme poverty, with most of the poverty burden found in Africa. Now people are living in more hunger than before with increases in food price becoming the next silent pandemic. That is why the UN Secretary General Antonio Guterres said: *"Unless we act now, the 2030 Agenda will become epitaph for a world that might have been."* Neither the capitalism nor communism can save humanity from the cancer of poverty or economic hardship that has engulfed the world except the Islamic economic principles. The social and economic principles of Islam are based on divine gift and with the present pathetic situation of humanity, only divine gift can save the world. This is because the social and economic principles of Islam are not man-made theories and principles that are only designed to exploit poor communities. A typical example is the case of Niger in Africa. After independent, France which is the colonial power kept controlling the social and economic policies of Niger to the extent that Niger was considered one of the poorest countries in the world but this country (Niger) is one of the major producers of uranium and recently has identified oil. The policy of France was exploiting this innocent country so that her nationals (French) would live fulfilling lives. This greedy capitalistic principle would not help the people of Niger. Although the new leaders didn't implement an Islamic form of economic and social principles, the economic and social lives of the people of Niger have improved significantly especially after they asked French to leave their country. Similarly, all these conflicts raging in Africa involving Boko Haram, Islamic State of Iraq and the Levant (ISIL), Al-Qaida, etc have been alleged to be sponsored by certain countries whose interest are for economic gains. The Islamic principles promote the sharing and care of the whole humanity with God-given natural resources and wealth. While the interest of the developed countries is on how to control the global natural resources, Islam on the other hand promotes the care of the whole of humanity and well-being of humanity. The Jews introduced the system of interest taking around the world and till date, the world economy is controlled by this greedy and evil practice where people are exploited by placing huge interests on innocent individuals. What we must always remember is human life is a divine gift and Islam is against any system that sucks the blood of poor people in the world as being done by some developed countries. To Islam, it is a religious duty upon the rich person to share his/her wealth with the poor thereby promoting spiritual, economic, social, and moral principles which in turn brings social cohesion.

Some would however argue with me that the social justice and equalities practices in these western countries are adequately implemented to the extent that the poor get their fair share of material benefits through social welfare and social security system. To a person who has never visited western countries, he/she thinks no one starves to death in these countries. As a friend once told me which I also agree with, in principle it seems the social and economic principles that was prescribed by Islam is being implemented in this western countries rather than Muslim countries and communities. The poor in the western countries are exposed to several financial assistance programs such as Jobseeker's allowance, incapacity benefit, statutory sick pay, disablement allowance, hardship loan, child benefits, family credit, etc. However, despite all these social interventions that have been developed by western countries, it has been reported that the gap between the rich and poor is widening at an alarming rate with the rich getting richer while the poor are getting poorer. When one visits a western country like UK, one would be shocked to see people who are so much stressed because the ripping off system turn people into zombies. In trains and buses, you see people who are so stressed out and living based on fears and anxiety because the economic system that was meant to protect them rather take advantage of them!

A DISUNITED PEOPLE (MUSLIMS)

Any community that is disunited will not be successful in its activities. That is why the Prophet of Islam (SAW) was so much concerned about the unity of Muslims. Islam has always advised Muslims to be united and act as one brotherhood who are in solidarity with one another. Before trying to synthesis the lack of unity and its effect on the Muslim community, let us put forward what the Quran and the Holy Prophet advised about unity and brotherhood. Later the teachings of great Islamic scholars would be evaluated in order to provide novel and practical solutions.

The Holy Prophet (SAW) said: *"Do not envy each other, do not outbid each other, do not hate each other, and do not outsell each other. Rather, be servant of Allah as brothers. The Muslim is the brother of another Muslims. He does not wrong him, nor humiliates him, nor look down upon him. Righteousness is here"* (and he pointed his chest three times).

And he (SAW) once said: *"It is enough evil for a man to look down upon his Muslim brother. The entirety of the Muslim is scared to another Muslim: his life, his wealth, and his reputation."* (Sahih Muslim 2564).

"Verily, the believers are like a structure, each part strengthening the other" and he (SAW) clasped his holy fingers together (Sahih Al-Bukhari).

"Three things are the best of acts; first, to treat people with equity and justice; second to assist your co-religionist brethren as fellows and aid them financially; and third, to remember God under all condition" (Bihar-al-Anwar, vol 74).

"He who begins his day without endeavouring for the improvement of Muslims affairs, is no Muslim" (Al Kafi, vol 2).

"Whoever fulfilled the needs of his brother, Allah will fulfil his needs; whoever brought his (Muslim) brother out of discomfort, Allah will bring him out of the discomfort of the Day of Resurrection (Sahih Al- Bukhari)

The Holy Quran also says:

"The believers are but brothers, so make settlements between your brothers. And fear Allah that you may receive mercy (49:10)."

"And hold fast by the covenant of Allah all together and be not disunited, and remember the favour of Allah on you when you were enemies, then He united your hearts so by His favours you became brethren; and you were on the brink of a pit of fire ... (3:103)."

"Indeed this, your religion (community), is one religion (community), and I am your Lord, so worship Me (21:92)

This advice should be enshrined as the charter of unity for Muslims. But what does Muslims understand by the word unity? To have practical understanding of what unity stands for, we must delve back into history and evaluate why Muslims were very successful during the time of the Prophet (SAW) by overcoming so many odds? Sometime when reading books on the sacrifices the early Muslims undertook for the religion to be where it is now, I shed tears. They fought wars where they were outnumbered but won, a typical example is the famous battle of Badr where they were outnumbered by 3 to 1 but these gallant men fought with one sense of purpose with everything in their blood that they overcame the odds against them. The battle of Badr took place on 17 Ramadan 2 AH. What is the spiritual lesson can we take from the battle of Badr which can shape the people of Muhammad (SAW)? We can find the answer in the Holy Quran where Allah (SWT) tells us

"Well, if you are steadfast and mindful of Allah, your Lord will reinforce you with five thousand swooping angels if the enemy should suddenly attack you" (3:125).

Here Allah is reminding us of His (SWT) assistance if we are steadfast and mindful of Him (SWT). One of the mindfulness of Allah's (SWT) is remaining united as recommended in Quran 49:10.

Before the battle of Badr, the companions of the Prophet (SAW) taught us the significant of unity. The model that Muslims needs now is the golden age of Islam when they were strong, unified, and free from corruption because of the presence of the best teacher and perfect role model they had in the Holy Prophet (SAW). During the early phase of Islam, Muslims had to endure horrific prosecution. When the people of Quraysh placed an embargo on them which led to the community been embargoed of business and societal dealings, it was the spirit of unity and perseverance that held their together and they never for once betrayed the call of Muhammad (SAW) to the religion of Allah. According to history, the persecution was so severe that Muhammad (SAW) advised them to migrate to the present Ethiopia and Eritrea. When the people of Quraysh sent emissary to the King, the Muslims remained united and elected one leader to be their voice. Through his unique presentation of Islam, they were allowed to stay. In Mecca, Muslims continued to be persecuted till emissary from Medina invited Muslims to migrate to Medina. The Medinites recommended to the Muhammad (SAW) as follows: *"The Jews of Medina had predicted the coming of a Prophet and that they were lucky to have a Prophet amongst them. In the past they had been told they were inferior to the Jews and the Christians as they were the people of the Book while they were not. They were therefore happy to have a Prophet who brought the Holy Quran, consisting of verses that inspired hearts and reformed human thoughts"*.

When the Muslims of Mecca migrated to Medina, the people referred to them as Ansar (meaning helpers) out of love and unity that cannot be described in plain language took these Muslims referred to as Muhajirun into their homes. An Ansar having more than one house gifted one to the Muhajirun. They established a brotherhood which was indestructible. This brotherhood was the first charter of Islamic unity and if the present generation of Muslims takes some moral lesion from this and hold this principle of brotherhood with sincerity and faith, a strong Muslim community would emerge.

This brotherhood had a foundation when Muhammad (SAW) gave the Medinites a promise when he (SAW) realised they harboured some fear that one day he might desert them and return to Mecca: *"O Muslim of Medina! Your blood is my blood and mine is yours. I belong to you and you to me. Whosoever intends to fight with you, will witness me his opponent; and in your fight for the Cause of Allah, you will find me with you."*

This was a strong bond between the people of Medina and Muslims represented by Muhammad (SAW) himself. But some would argue that this is about war. My answer is yes but you would know your real brother during your period of adversary! Helping a Muslim brother is a sign of faith and that unity is best rope that will hold Muslims together. In fulfilling an all aspect of brotherhood, we (Muslims) must make provision for mistakes for which we must be ready to forgive.

This was further confirmed by Allah:

"The believers are nothing else than brothers. So make reconciliation between brothers, and fear Allah, that you may receive mercy" (49:10).

In the above verse, Allah (SWT) directs Muslims to be brothers to one another and when there is any misunderstanding, we should reconcile so that we receive the mercy of Allah (SWT). But what is our status now? Muslims do not regard themselves as brothers to even of reconcile. This is contrary to the advice given by Muhammad (SAW) who said:

"Muslim is the brother of another Muslim, so he never oppresses him, does not stop helping him, and does not let him down in the face of events ..."

In another he (SAW) said:

'... two believing brothers are the same as two hands washing each other, so they have perfect cooperation, and make allowance for each other's faults ...'

Imam Ali bin Talib who is a symbol of knowledge also added: '... *the best brother is the one who is less considerate in advice and guidance ...* 'He also said: '... *your best brother is the one who is angry with you in the way of truth ...* 'While in another sermon, he (AS) said: '... *the best brother is the one who does not make his brothers need others ...* ' In this last sermon,

Imam Ali (AS) set the perfect standard for brotherhood when he (AS) advised:*"Do not allow your brother (Muslim) become dependent on others. Help them when they are in need."*

During the Last sermon of the Prophet (SAW), he gave the ultimate advice on brotherhood when he (SAW) said:

> *"O people! Listen to my words and understand them. You must know that a Muslim is the brother of another Muslim, and they form one brotherhood. Nothing of his brother his lawful for a Muslim except what he himself allows willingly. So you should not oppress one another ..."*

How do we claim we are Muslims yet not following the recommendation of Muhammad (SAW).

Finally, in the Quran Allah has this strong advice for us (Muslims) that if we not hold tight to the rope of brotherhood, we would lose courage and power.

> **"Obey Allah and His Messenger and do not quarrel with one another lest you should lose courage and your power departs. Be steadfast, surely Allah is with those who remain steadfast"** (4:59).

We would as the Prophet (SAW) predicted be having large number but weak. Is this not the present condition of Muslims? The concept of brotherhood is meant not for only Muslims but any progressive society needs to establish unity to enable it achieve it societal goals. As an African, I am always sad with the lack of unity in Africa. If Africans can follow the societal medicine that Muhammad (SAW) prescribed, Africa would become a united continent which would serve her people well instead of seeing her children travel to Europe, UK, America, etc where they are treated like non-humans beings!

This brotherhood was first established when Allah said:

> **"Allah created you from a single being and out of it created its mate, Adam and his wife; and out of the two spread many men and women ..."** (3:1)

In this verse Allah (SWT) is reminding humanity that we are from one common ancestry from the same source. This means we are only divided on the basis of piety (goodness) or evilness. In a society where brotherhood is held high in esteem, there is social security. When we have a viable Muslim brotherhood, we would be protected from the harm of disunity and integrity would be preserve. This would lead to unity, love, and cooperation among Muslims and social balance can be properly shaped. Brotherhood based on religion has certain advantages over brotherhood based on interest such as racial, socioeconomic partners, political, etc. This is the most common brotherhood promoted by Western philosophers and political system. In this type of brotherhood, the real spirit of brotherhood is not created and an individual looks for personal gains instead of mutual benefits. That is why to the USA, they do not have a permanent friend but permanent interest. This means in brotherhood of socioeconomic with the Americans, when they exhaust what they want from such union, they discard the brotherhood. This is true with most advanced nations! However, in Muslim brotherhood, we would be guided by faith where no one considers another inferior. This was captured clearly in "Ayat of Brotherhood" when the Prophet (SAW) established brotherhood among his (SAW) companions.

The advantage of Muslims brotherhood is it changes the situation of Muslims. Of interest to this author is respect for human dignity. As Muslims, we must respect not only Muslims but non-Muslims; irrespective of their race, social status, and gender. In the Quran, many verses outline how Allah (SWT) honours humans. When He (SWT) created man, He (SWT) asked the angels to bow before man but Satan refused thinking he was superior to man. Because of that single act, Satan lost the favour he was enjoying in paradise culminating in him been driven out of paradise. He vowed to destroy human beings by making them disobedient to Allah. The first battle of man was against Satan which should be the focus of an ideal Muslim brotherhood.

How do we solve the problems encountering Muslims?

First with have to start with what can be referred to as the "fulcrum of Muslims disunity": Shia and Sunni division.

The division between Shiite and Sunni Muslims is regarded as the divisive knife within Muslims. We should not regard these ideological differences as the root of disunity among Islam because Muhammad (SAW) told us that division among Muslims is a blessing from Allah. It is this division that portrays Islam as religion of Knowledge because one is allowed to seek for knowledge and make a derivation from what he learns. If he makes a mistake, he will be honoured for trying to understand. The Shiite and Sunni branches of Islam were due to disagreements over who should rightfully succeed the Holy Prophet (SAW) after his (SAW) deaths. The current plight of Muslims around the world should be a sincere objective that should make any sincere Muslims sit up and agree that this Shiite and Sunni division must end. We have too many problems on our hands to continue disagreeing over an issue that has ideological root. Shiite and Sunni Muslims are one! So Shiite Muslims should not regard Sunni Muslims as their enemies vice versa. Therefore the happiness that greeted the cooperation between Iran and Saudi Arabia in 2023 cannot be explained. All right thinking Muslim should thank the Republic of China and Russia for bringing together the two powerful Islamic nations together.

What we should all understand is the common declaration that holds all Muslims together is the Kalimatu Shahada. Therefore we should love one another for the sake of Allah as outlined when Muhammad (SAW) said: *"There will be round Throne on the Day of Judgement, whose faces will be like the full moon; and when the people will be scared, they will not be scared, and when the people will fear, and they will not be scare, and when the people will fear, they will not fear; they are the devotees of Allah upon whom there shall be no fear, and they will not grieve."*

He was asked: *"Who are those O Messenger of Allah?"* He (SAW) said: *"They are those who love each other for the Sake of Allah Almighty."* Another sermon, he (SAW) said: *"There is no two persons who love each other for the Sake of Allah but that the dearer of them to Allah Almighty is the one who loves his companion more."*

It this unique love among the earlier Muslims that saw them conquered problems more difficult and more complex than this generation.

Allah told Jesus (AS):

"Were you to worship me much as is equal to the entire inhabitants of the heavens and earth, but without loving anyone for the Sake of Allah, your worship would not avail you in the least."

In this advice to Dawud (AS), Allah (SWT) said:

"Deal with people of the world according to the conduct of the world, and deal with people of the hereafter according to the conduct of the hereafter."

There is this famous narration between Allah (SWT) and Musa (AS) where Allah (SWT) asked Musa (AS):

"Have you ever done a deed for Me?" and he answered: *"O God! I have prayed for You, observed fasts, paid almsgiving, and practiced regular charity."*

Allah answered him:

"The prayer will be a proof in your favour. Fasting is a shield to protect you. Almsgiving is a shade to safeguard you. And the obligatory charity is light to guide you to the truth. Which deed than have you done for My Sake?"

Musa (AS) asked:

"O my God! Guide me to a deed which is to be for Your Sake?"

He (SWT) said:

"O Musa! Have you ever taken for friend anyone for My Sake? Have you ever taken for enemy anyone for My Sake"?

Musa (AS) then realised the best deeds is loving and hating for the sake of Allah. Then we also let the love of Muhammad (SAW) to be our path to the love of Allah!

Next, we should increase our sense of responsibilities as outlined by helping one another. The earlier Muslims withstood the tests of times because they were always there to help one another. In a unique sermon, Muhammad (SAW) said:

"The rights of the Muslim upon the Muslim are six, "When you meet him give him the greeting of peace, when he invites you, respond to his invitation, when he seeks your advice, advise him, when he sneezes and praises Allah, supplicate for mercy upon him, when he becomes ill, visit him, and when he dies to follow him (for his funeral)."

This is the best responsibility of a Muslim upon his fellow Muslim brothers and sisters. In this complex world, humans depend on the skills of other people in various fields for our survival. Therefore in our societies, we have two types of responsibilities, responsibilities to your Muslim brethren and that of non-Muslims, our brethren in creation as outlined by Ali Ibn Talib (AS). We should not regard our non-Muslims brethren as our enemies because we as Muslims cannot carry our societal activities alone. Sheikh Abdul Hakim, a well renowned British Muslim scholar reminded us when he wrote:

"To solve the problem thrown at us and at our identity by the real world outside the mosque gates, we (Muslims) need to engage regularly with non-Muslim society. People convert through personal experience of Muslims. And this takes place overwhelmingly, at the workplace. Other social contexts are closed to us: the pub, the beach, the office party. But work is a prime environment for being noticed, and judged, as Muslims. There is nothing remotely new in this. Islam has always spread primarily through social interactions connected with work. The early Muslims who conquered half of the world did not set up soapboxes in the town squares of Alexandria, Cordoba, Fez, in the hope that Christians would flock to them and hear their preaching. They did business with the Christians; and their nobility and integrity of conduct won the Christians over. That is the model followed by Muslims; and it is the one that we must retain today, by interacting with non-Muslims in our places of work, as much as we can."

Therefore a Muslim should guide the society to Islam by being righteous, fight atrocities and encourage virtue, enjoining good, helping people, and trying to win the public opinion while trying to win the public over to the side of Islam. The task won't be easy but as my grandma used to advice me: *"Nothing good comes easy."*

Let us be good servant of Islam! One of the unique characters of Muhammad (SAW) is that he (SAW) is Al-Amin therefore Muslims must follow his (SAW) footsteps and condemn any form of intolerance which has given Islam bad name.

With our Muslim brethren, we must be guided by the advice of Muhammad (SAW) who said*: "No one of you shall become a true believer until he desires for his brother what he desires for himself.* (Buhkari Muslim*)."*

From this beautiful advice, our Light (SAW) tells us if you don't want to be sick, wish your brethren the same; when you don't want any nation to attack you, when you see a brute nation attacking your Muslim brethren then go and help them! Furthermore, Muhammad (SAW) told us: *"A Muslim is the brother of a Muslims; he does him no wrong, nor does he let him down, nor does he despise him. Fear of God is here, fear of God is here* (and he pointed to his chest*). It is evil enough that a Muslim should look down on his brother. For every Muslim is scared to one another: his blood, his honour, and his property. Allah does not look at your bodies or your forms, or your deeds, but also He looks at your hearts.* (Bukhari, Muslim)."

In this wonderful sermon, the Prophet (SAW) offers a unique solution to Muslims: the world is full of jealousy, selfishness, and backbiting and through this sermon, he (SAW) offered solutions for Muslims. One adorable trait of Muhammad (SAW) is his love for Muslims. He (SAW) always thought of his people. The world now is filled with all the negative traits (of jealousy, selfishness, and backbiting) therefore we as Muslims should have sense of fraternity so that we come to one common platform which would lead to the advancement of Muslims!

Allah tells us:

"Invite people to the way of your Lord, with wisdom and beautiful preaching, and argue with them in a ways that are the best and most gracious. For your Lord knows best who have strayed from His Path, and who receive guidance. (16:125)"

In this verse, Allah advises that the best way to call people to good is using your wisdom and beautiful talks. In this modern world when the younger and future generations of Islam are exposed to all kind of vices, this is the best strategy to direct them to the straight path.

The type of brotherhood we should develop should not be based on frequently attempting to harm non-Muslims. We have to remember that Muslims of the past used justice, honesty, integrity, kindness, sincerity, and truthfulness as mantra which drew millions of non-Muslims to the religion. That is why he (SAW) recommended: *"You enjoin the good, forbid the evil, and believe in Allah. (3:110)."*

The Prophet (SAW) gave a sterling description of Muslims: *"You find the Muslims in their mutual love and compassion, like one body, should any organ of it fall ill, the rest of the body will share in the fever and sleeplessness that ensues."*

Till Muslims start acting as one body, we will remain disunited and when we are disunited we will be weak and the smallest army will defeat us!

Finally, we must remember this verse from Allah (SWT):

"Everyone's God-given human dignity must be respected, regardless of his or her faith, race, ethnic origin, gender, and social status. (17:70)"

MODERN EVENTS THAT IMPACTED ISLAM & LESSONS FROM THEM

❈

Over the course of history, humanity has faced some defining moments that shaped world. We can think of French Revolution, World War (WW) 1 and WWII, Nazi Germany, Russian Revolution, fall of the Berlin wall, the dropping of atomic bomb on Hiroshima, Indian Revolution, Establishment of Maoist in China, Assassination of John F Kennedy, 9/11 Attack in USA, and COVID-19 pandemic. These events shock the world. COVID-19 was first reported in 2019 from Wuhan, China and the impact was devastating with human and economic consequences which the world is still working hard to overcome while writing this book. In Islam, there are some events that changed global perspective of the religion.

The Islamic Republic of Iran's revolution

In March 1979, there was a referendum Iran in which 98% of the populace voted to opt for an Islamic Republic. It was a revolution that shook the world and led to redrawing of global alliance. In December, Ayatollah Khomeini (RA) emerged as the Supreme Leader of the Islamic Republic of Iran and he (RA) developed the concept of *velayat-e-faqih* (guardianship based on jurist). This concept is based on the fact that religious jurist are best qualified for leadership and should have oversight over the government. In support of the concept, Khomeini (RA) said:

"When anyone studies a little or pays little attention to the rules of Islamic government, Islamic politics, Islamic society, and Islamic economy he will realize that Islam is a very political religion. Anyone who will say that religion is separate from politics is a fool; he does not know Islam or politics."

In another speech, he (RA) said:*"The fundamental difference between Islamic government, on the one hand, and constitutional monarchy and republic, on the other, is this: whereas the representatives of the people or the monarch in such regimes engage in legislation, in Islam the legislative power and competence to establish laws belongs exclusively to God Almighty."*

This concept set Iran against the Western world and some countries in the Middle East. On the eve of the Iranian New Year on March 21, 1980, Khomeini (RA) sent a defiant message to the world when he said: *"We shall confront the world with our ideology."*

In a statement about the revolution, Ayatollah Khomeini (RA) assured the world: *"We shall export our revolution to the whole world. Until the cry 'There is no god but Allah' resounds over the whole world, there will be struggle. If you have divine motives, material benefits will follow suit but they are no longer material; they have become divine."*

This concept led to the Shiite-Sunni friction widens and certain Western political system took advantage and influenced Saddam Hussein who by then regarded himself as leader of Sunni Muslims led Iraq to attack Iran. But the mistake the Western system made was they didn't accept that in Iran, a new regional heavyweight had emerged and destroying it was not going to be easy. The invasion of Iran by Saddam's army did not weaken the resolve of Khomeini (RA) and his people but rather strengthened the revolution and made Iranians more determined to carry the revolution outside their country. This further created panic in those who opposed the revolution especially when Iran adopted a national slogan: *"Neither East nor West"* which made the country an independent ideological entity that did not depend on the East and West

With time, the influence of the Islamic Republic of Iran reached far and wide as well as building their strength and influence. It is now considered as one of the heavyweight in Middle East and beyond. This impacted global geopolitics in which Iran became a major player. One of the effects of the Islamic Revolution was and still America's hostility to Iran. This hostility can be linked to the hostage crisis where the revolutionaries took

52 Americans and barricaded them for 444 days in the US embassy in Tehran. This hostage crisis was a bottleneck and as Boroujerdi said: *"It is fair to say that Washington was beginning to get worried about the anti-status-quo message of the Iranian revolution even before the hostages were taken, but the hostage crisis was a game-changer."*

Till date, US political system remained shocked by that event. Stephen Kinzer explained: *"The American political class has never recovered from the shock and humiliation of the hostage crisis. It cast Iran as the face of evil in many American hearts."* But to some Muslim revolutionaries such as Ibrahim Al-Zazzaki of Nigeria, Hassan Nasrallah, this author, etc, it gave them the ideological basis for their stance.

Why is the revolution of Iran so important? The hostage taking and bringing down of the Shah dynasty who was then regarded as one of the closest allies to the US turned heads to Iran. It created the belief that even the most prominent ally of a super power could not withstand the revolution of the people. This created further panic across the Middle East whose form of rule was similar to the Shah. The revolution also turned Iran into the flag bearer of countries that were hostile to the US and the Europeans Union (which then included UK). Iran became so influential to the extent that no country or group was so threatening to US and its allies like Iran. The revolution changed the political culture. Khomeini's slogan of *"exporting the Islamic revolution"* to other countries especially the Islamic world was a game changer. It must be noted that the US and its allies panicked that if the revolution should be exported to other countries it would have dire consequences not only in Middle East but also some states in eastern Europe and developing countries that were dependent on the superpowers would start demanding for economic and socio-political independence. Islamic Republic of Iran is still a pivot in the fight against any form of Western dominance which has continuously been a source of animosity between Iran and the Western political system. In the past, Iran regarded all Western countries as enemies but currently; Iran, Russia, China, Saudi Arabia, Egypt and other BRICS countries have formed an alliance that is threatening the dominance of the US. All reasonable thinking people should positively hope that this alliance achieve its objective!

In the Muslim world, the revolution had profound effect. The *"exporting of the revolution to neighbouring countries and across the Muslim world"* was a very well planned strategy as Iran exported the concept of the revolution to other Muslim countries. He (Khomeini) further called for confrontation with the Western powers who he often referred to as "Great Satan" and made the liberation of the occupied territories as one of the priorities. They (Iranians) also focused on issues that were dear to Muslims and other freedom fighters: Palestine and pan-Islamism. Communication strategies were effectively used in order to export the ideals of the revolution across not only Middle East and Muslim countries but the entire world so that the newly formed Islamic leadership would be solidified. But it must be noted that the Islamic Revolution didn't result in the creation of Islamic Caliphate but rather the formation of new Islamic "order" in which dissatisfied Muslim communities who were looking for political and economic changes were trained. This order also had profound effect on developing countries that also realised that they needed similar changes. By attempting to export the revolution's concept, the Islamic Republic of Iran tried to focus attention on one principle of the religion and political development: Islamic fundamentalism. That was why Khomeini (RA) referred to the person who tried to separate religion and politics as lacking wisdom. This Islamic fundamentalism which started in Iran moved to Southeast Asia, Middle East, and North Africa. Some Muslims in other part of Africa especially West Africa started associating themselves to the ideals of the revolution. This was very significant as by then Muslims seems to have lost the pride associated to been a Muslim. But the effect might have even surprised Khomeini himself as explained by Osman Tarek: *"It is highly doubtful that Khomeini ever thought his system would be expanded to Egypt, Syria, Morocco, Malaysia, Pakistan, and the Sunni Islamic countries. But the notion of the rise of Islamic scholars to command their societies sounded to him not only possible but an Islamic obligation."* There is a general consensus that the Arab Spring had some influence of the revolution but I would not be discussing the Arab Spring in this book as a form of respect for the late Muammar Gaddafi of Libya. An important lesson Muslims should learn from the Islamic Republic of Iran is we MUST be dependent on only Allah's Mercy and Guidance but not putting our hope in any Western ideology. When we have divine hope, Muslims would become a force again!

September 11 2001

> *"We cannot turn against one another by letting this fight*
> *defined as a war between America and Islam"*
>
> > - President Barack Obama

The devastating impact of September 11, 2001 cannot be forgotten. While the human and economic costs were high, for Muslims and Islam, it was both positive and negative. After the attack on the Twin Towers and Pentagon, many Muslims in America became targets of anger and racism with Islamophobia increased to the extent that some individuals were beaten, attacked or held at gunpoint simply because they were perceived to be Muslims. In an interview on ABC News, Rep Ilhan Omar said: "As Americans, as people who are living here, we were also attacked. This is our community, this is our country, and there were Muslims who lost their lives in those towers, who were Muslim fire-fighters, who lost their lives." According to the data, hate crime against Muslims rose 167% from 2000 to 2001. With increasing hate against Muslims growing, then President George W. Bush made an appeal: "The face of terror is not the true faith of Islam." Sally Howell, the director of the Center for American Studies at the University of Michigan also said: " In the post 9/11 period, there was a lot of fear about Muslims and terrorisms in the United States and so we created all these opportunities to surveil and harass citizens and even entrap citizens in our desire to fight terrorism." Some politicians took hate against Muslims as tool to the extent that in March 2015, Trump alleged on CNN that hatred defines the Islamic faith saying *"I think Islam hates us. There's something there that-there's a tremendous hatred there. There's a tremendous hatred. We have to get to the bottom of it. There's an unbelievable hatred of us."* Immediately after 9/11, about 60% of Americans reported having unfavourable attitudes towards Islam while many America Muslims and Islam with fear-associated terms such as violence, fanatics, radical, war, and terrorism. These views which resonated across the US caught the attention of not only non-Muslim Americans but around the world September 11 though sad had some positive impact on Islam. It was without doubt one of the defining moments of the 21st century till present. According to Pew Research Center, they found during a survey that most Americans didn't know about Islam and Muslims, or admitted to not knowing anything about Islam and Muslims. Dr Besheer Mohamed, a senior researcher at Pew Research Center remarked "The public has fairly limited sort of direct knowledge or interaction with Muslims." September 11 therefore saw Americans increasing their attention to religious and spiritual issues. Although a study by Uecker didn't find remarkable religious revival among young adults, other research involving Americans who wanted to study Islam showed increased curiosity of Islam. Although America Muslims report of facing discrimination and questions about their national loyalty, knowledge about Islam increased not only in the US but around the world. A positive exposure Islam received after 9/11 was almost all the international media were discussing Islam. Now academic institutes have incorporated Islam in their curriculums, and there are many interfaith initiatives that are bringing Muslims, Christians and Jews together. Islam is on the rise around the world for after 9/11, non-Muslims started asking questions which led them to read Islamic books like the Quran, Hadith, etc. From their research, they began converting to Islam as feared by the Western Philosophers. Apart from high conversion rate, 9/11 awakens Muslims that they need to have interest in electoral politics. In the US, individuals likes Ilhan Omar, Mussab Ali and Rashida Tlaib were elected to Congress. However, it must be mentioned that 9/11 also saw some Muslims leaving the religion because they wanted to hide their identities.

JESUS (AS) OF ISLAM

Unknown to majority of Christians, Jesus (AS) is one of the most powerful Prophets in Islam while most Muslims don't know that refusing to believe in the Prophethood of Jesus (AS) leads to one leaving the religion of Islam. Two issues that differentiate the Muslims' view of Jesus (AS) from Christians' view are "Jesus being God" and "Jesus dying for the sins of humanity." These issues have generated so much debate but in a world where religion is being used as business tool, nobody wants to understand the Muslims' stance even when the Bible is used in debates. Based on this, I will try to use Quranic and Biblical narrations to address the issue of Jesus (AS).

There are about 37 verses in the Holy Quran that spoke about Jesus (AS) from his birth to death and whether he (AS) ever stated he (AS) was God. The Quran verse on the birth of Jesus (AS) is found in:

"And remember the one who guarded her chastity, so We breathed into her through Our angel, Gabriel, making her and her son a sign for all peoples. *[21:91]*"

In this verse, Allah (SWT) told us that Mary (AS) the mother of Jesus (AS) was chastity woman who was visited by Archangel Jibril (AS) to inform her of the decision of Allah (SWT) to bless her with a powerful prophet. The miracle here was Mary (AS) was not married and never had sexual relationship before her encounter with Jibril (AS). After giving birth to Jesus (AS), Mary (AS) became distressed and while crying remarked:

56

"Would that I had died before this, and had been forgotten and out of sight (19:23)."

The Quran gave a clear message about the birth of Jesus (AS):

> **"Behold! The angels said: 'O Mary! Allah giveth thee glad tidings of a Word from Him: his name will be Messiah-Christ Eesa, the son of Mary, held in honour in this world and the Hereafter and of (the company of) those nearest to God/Allah … (3:45)."**

This verse was confirmed by the Bible:

> **"Therefore the Lord himself shall give you a sign; Behold, a virgin shall conceive, and bear a son, and shall call his name Immanuel (Isaiah 7: 14)."**

> **"Behold, a virgin shall be with child, and shall bring forth a son, and they shall call his name Emmanuel, which being interpreted is, God with us. (Mathew 1:23)."**

On the conception of Jesus (AS), the Quran gave a vivid description of how he (AS) would be conceived:

> **"And Mary the daughter of 'Imran, who guarded her chastity; & We breathed into (her body) of Our spirit; & she testified to the truth of the words of her Lord & of His Revelations, & was one of the devout (servants) (66:12)."**

> **"Relate in the Book about Mary, when she withdrew from her family to a place in the East. She placed a screen from them; then we sent our Angel (Gabriel) and he appeared before her as a man in all respects (19: 16-17)."**

The first attestation made by Jesus (AS) is clearly captured in the Quran: *"I am0 truly a servant of Allah. He has destined me to be given the*

Scripture and to be a prophet. He has made me a blessing wherever I go, and bid me to establish prayer and give alms-tax as long as I live, and to be kind to my mother. He has not made me arrogant or defiant. Peace be upon me the day I was born, the day I die, and the day I will be raised back to life!" That is Jesus, son of Mary. And this is a word of truth, about which they dispute. **[19:30-34]**.

Then he also had this: *"Surely Allah is my Lord and your Lord, so worship Him alone. This is the Straight Path."* **[19:36]**.

So if Jesus (AS) made this excellent attestation, why did and does some Christians hold the belief that Jesus (AS) is God? The answer lies in the miracle of his (AS) birth. In an answer to this belief, Allah (SWT) outlined in the Quran:

> **"The Day when Allah will say, 'O Jesus, Son of Mary, remember My favour upon you and upon your mother when I supported you with the Pure Spirit and you spoke to the people in the cradle and in maturity; and remember when I taught you writing and wisdom and the Torah and the Gospel; and when you designed from clay what was like the form of a bird with My permission, then you breathed into it, and it became a bird with My permission; and you healed the blind and the leper with My permission; and when you brought forth the dead with My permission; and when I restrained the Children of Israel from killing you when you came to them with clear proofs and those who disbelieved among them said, 'This is not but obvious magic (5: 110)."**

This clearly shows that Jesus (AS) was favoured by Allah (SWT) due to that he performed so many miracles. The inability of Jesus (AS) do things on his (AS) own is clearly stated in the Bible where he (AS) said: *"I can do nothing on my own initiative. As I hear, I judge; and my judgment is just, because I do not seek my own will, but the will of Him who sent me* (John 5:30)."

In this verse, Jesus (AS) told his disciples of his infallibility and depended on a supreme power (SWT) to enable him performs miraculous deeds. Jesus (AS) is a chosen prophet who is regarded as one of the powerful Prophets (AS) in Islam. That is why the Quran made reference of Jesus (AS) as Prophet:

"That is Jesus, son of Mary-the word of truth about which they are in dispute (19:34)."

Jesus (AS) gave an excellent testimony when he (AS) said: *"He (Jesus) said: Verily! I am a slave of Allah, He has given me the Scripture and made me a Prophet (19:30)."*

In another clear verse, Allah (SWT) told us:

"Indeed, We gave Moses the Book and sent after him successive messengers. And We gave Jesus, son of Mary, clear proofs and supported him with the Holy Spirit. Why is it that every time a messenger comes to you ˈIsraelitesˈ with something you do not like, you become arrogant, rejecting some and killing others? *[2:87]."*

Here we are told that two of the powerful Prophets (AS): Moses and Jesus were given favours by Allah (SWT). While Moses (AS) was given the book, Jesus was given clear proofs and was supported with the Holy Spirit. Who supported him? God by sending His guidance through Jibril (AS).

This verse is confirmed in the Bible:

" ... crowd said, 'this is the Prophet Jesus of Nazareth of Galilee. (Matthew 21:11)."

"And he said, 'He is a Prophet (John 9:17)."

All these verses support the Muslims' argument that Jesus (AS) was a Prophet of Allah. But was he (AS) God?

In the Quran, Jesus (AS) told his followers: *"O Children of Israel-worship God, my Lord and your Lord (5:72)."*

In another verse, he (AS) said: *"Say: He is God the One and Only; And there is none like unto Him (111: 1 and 4)."*

These verses are supported by the Bible: *"The most important commandment is this: Hear, O Israel; the Lord our God is one Lord.* (Mark 12: 29)."* And in another verse outlined: *"You are right in saying that God is one and there is no other but him* Mark 12: 32)."

Who is Jesus (AS)? The answer is Jesus (AS) is a messenger of Allah.

In the Quran,

"Those who follow the messenger, the unlettered Prophet, whom they find mentioned in their own (scriptures) in the law (Torah) and the Gospel (Injeel) (7:157)."

"And remember. Jesus, the son of Mary. Said: O Children of Israel! I am the messenger of Allah (Sent) to you, confirming the Law (Torah) before me, and giving glad tidings of a messenger to come after me, whose name is AHMAD (Praiseworthy) ... (61:6)."

These verses are supported by the Biblical verses:

"When the Spirit of truth comes, he will guide you into all the truth, for he will not speak on his own authority, but whatever he hears he will speak, and he will declare to you the things that are to come. 'He will glorify Me, for He will take of Mine and will disclose it to you (John 16:13)."

That is why the Prophet (SAW) referred to Jesus (AS) as:

"I am most close to Jesus, son of Mary, among the whole of mankind in this worldly life and the next life. They said: Allah's Messenger how is it? Thereupon he said: Prophets are brothers in faith, having different mothers. Their religion is, however, one and there is no Apostle between us (between I and Jesus)."

In Quranic verse, Allah has this strong message for humanity:

> **"O People of the Book! Do not go to extremes regarding your faith; say nothing about Allah except the truth. The Messiah, Jesus, son of Mary, was no more than a messenger of Allah and the fulfilment of His Word through Mary and a spirit created by a command from Him. So believe in Allah and His messengers and do not say, "Trinity." Stop!—for your own good. Allah is only One God. Glory be to Him! He is far above having a son! To Him belongs whatever is in the heavens and whatever is on the earth. And Allah is sufficient as a Trustee of Affairs."** *[4:171]*

All these verses significantly show that Jesus (AS) was a messenger of God. But if by the virtue of him (AS) been born without father makes him (AS) a god, then how should we refer to Melchizedek who were described as: "Without father, without mother, without genealogy, having neither beginning of days nor end of life …" in Hebrew 7:3? He didn't have a beginning or ending which meant he was neither born nor did he die! If we are to follow the logic of Christendom then it means Melchizedek was greater than Jesus (AS). But to us Muslims, Jesus (AS) was greater than Melchizedek because Jesus (AS) is regarded as one of the powerful Prophets of God. Finally, how do we classify Adam (AS) because he also didn't have a father and mother?

God is to be worshipped. Did Jesus (AS) worshipped God or was he (AS) a deity who was worshipped? Both the Quran and Bible made significant reference to this.

In the Quran Allah (SWT) told us:

> **"O Maryam, (Mary) be devout to your Lord, and prostrate yourself and bow down with the ones who bow down (for Him)"** (3:43).

> **"While Jesus has said, 'O Children of Israel-worship God, my Lord and your Lord"** (5:72).

In these verses, Jesus was recommended to prostrate to his Lord and also he (AS) advised the Children of Israel to worship God. These verses were confirmed in the Bible:

> *"He (Jesus) advanced a little and fell on his face (prostration) and prayed, saying, 'O my Father" (Mathew 26:39).*

Finally, was Jesus crucified? The crucifixion of Jesus is the foundation of Christianity to the extent that some argue that without crucifixion, there would be no Christianity. While majority of Christians hold the belief that Jesus (AS) died for the sin of humanity, the Quranic and Biblical arguments have different narrative. In the Quran, Allah revealed:

> **"...and for boasting, "We killed the Messiah, Jesus, son of Mary, the messenger of Allah." But they neither killed nor crucified him—it was only made to appear so. Even those who argue for this crucifixion are in doubt. They have no knowledge whatsoever—only making assumptions. They certainly did not kill him"** *[4:157].*

In this verse, Allah told us that they did not kill Jesus for it was made to appear so.

In the Bible, similar fact was stated:

> *"You will only observe with your eyes and see the punishment of the wicked. If you make the Most High your dwelling— even the LORD, who is my refuge-then no harm will befall you, no disaster will come near your tent. For he will command his angels concerning you to guard you in all your ways; they will lift you up in their hands, so that you will not strike your foot against a stone. You will tread upon the lion and the cobra; you will trample the great lion and the serpent. Because he loves me," says the LORD, "I will rescue him; I will protect him, for he acknowledges my name. He will call upon me, and I will answer him; I will be with him in trouble, I will deliver him and honour him. With long life will I satisfy him and show him my salvation." (Psalm 91: 8-16) (I strategically underlined some part)*

Allah promised protecting him (Jesus). On the cross, the man crucified lamented: *"God, why have You forsaken me!"* If it was Jesus (AS), God won't forsake him (AS) for God said:

"He will call upon Me, and I will answer him; I will be with him in trouble, I will deliver him and honour him"

In Luke 4:10-12, it was clearly stated:

"For the Scriptures say, 'He will order his angels to protect and guard you. And they will hold you up with their hands so you won't even hurt your foot on a stone."

The Scriptures also say, 'You must not test the Lord your God.'"

In these verses, God was giving Jesus His promise. So was that promise fulfilled or not? To us Muslims, Jesus was the righteous man so God answered his prayers!

But hold on, let's go to Deuteronomy 21:23 which states: *"He who is hanged [i.e., either on a gallows or crucified] is accursed of God."* Come on my Christian siblings! How can you associate Jesus (AS) with a punishment that incurred the curse of God? It is blasphemy to even think Jesus (AS) was crucified! The Gospel of Barnabas stated that Jesus was not crucified but he (AS) ascended to heaven before the Romans could capture him (AS). Although some considered Barnabas' assertion as hoax, we need to understand the Barnabas was the disciple who was very close to Jesus (AS) therefore any testimony he (AS) renders should be taking in the court of argument!

ISLAM, THE PAN-GLOBAL RELIGION: HOPE FOR THE WORLD

❖

There are two major religions in the world: Islam and Christianity. However, some western philosophers have attempted without success to classify philosophy as a religion. In addition to these two major religions, there are also some religions/beliefs that are associated with certain communities such as Buddhism, Hindiusm, Judaism, Folk religions, Shintoism, Taoism, Baha'i, Confucianism, Jainism, and Sikhism. Furthermore, there are some categories of people who do not believe in any religion. Although religion is regarded as "God-sent", there are still some individuals who hold the believe that religion impedes the development of humanity, some also sees religion as source of social conflict, inequality, and violence. Still others think that with advances in science which provides answers to most questions, religion is outdated which is irrational and an impediment to scientific or human progress. Furthermore, some views religion as political tool used for social control and that religion can be a source of immoral acts or customs. Criticism of religion started decades along. Titus Lucretius who was a Roman poet believed that religion was born as a result of fear and ignorance and when the natural world is understood, humanity would be freed from the shackles of religion. Although he wasn't against religion itself, he held the belief that traditional religion is a superstition that is used by god to interfere with the world. A philosopher Al-Ma'arri also termed the statements of prophets' as fabrication, and branded God as a hypocrite for forbidding murder but send angels to end human's life. Another philosopher Voltaire was very critical of religious intolerance and he complained about Jews killing other Jews for simple worshipping a golden calf and also condemned Christians for killing other Christians over religious differences. To Voltaire, the real reasons for these killings were that Christians wanted to plunder the wealth of those killed. Islam was not spared criticism of Voltaire who was extremely critical of Muslim intolerance towards other religions. A Scottish philosopher, David Hume argued the philosophical basis of religion were not sound. He therefore argued that natural explanations for the order in the universe were reasonable. The early 21st century saw the emergence of new breed of modern criticism of religions; for example Daniel Dennett focused all his energy on trying to answer the question "why we believe strange things". A biologist Richard Dawkins suggested that God is delusional in his book while Christopher Hitchens held the belief that religion attack human dignity and argued that there is so much corruption in religious organizations. Philosophers have put forward series of hypothesis as their basis for their criticism of religion. These include viewing religion as a social construct which is just another form of human ideology. To others such as David Hume, religion is nothing but unsophisticated form of reasoning. This to these students of thought is due to the fact that most religions were formulated when the origin of life, the physiology of the body, and the nature of stars and planets were poorly understood. One intriguing criticism was put forward by Sam Harris who compared religion to mental illness and argued that "religion allows otherwise normal human beings to reap the fruit of madness and consider them holy". In a retrospective study that evaluated Abraham, Moses, Jesus Christ, and the Apostle Paul, the researchers hypothesised these gallant men of God may have had psychotic disorders that contributed to the inspirations for their revelation. They concluded that people with such disorders have had a monumental influence on civilization. Others have associated religion with inadequate medical care, honour killings and stoning, and genital modification and mutilation. Religious terrorism has been used against religion with some researchers arguing that terrorists are partially reassured by their religious views that they are supported and rewarded for their actions. Finally, religion has been criticised for suppressing scientific progress with the controversies over use of birth control, challenging research into embryonic stem cells and the theological objections to vaccination, anaesthesia, and blood transfusion as examples of religion suppressing scientific advances.

Is religion detrimental to humanity? In his book Is Religion Dangerous?, Keith Ward argued that not all false opinions can be termed delusional and that the belief of God is different as many great minds and people who live ordinary lives and believe in God are not irrational people. Some studies have shown that there are positive association between religion, moral behaviour and altruism while others showed that there are associations between religion and charity giving as recommended by Islam. It can also be argued that some religious violence are confused with religious moral rules and behaviour with non-religious factors. Events such as terrorists bombing should not be regarded as religious but rather politically motivated. In his argument, Mark Juergensmeyer was of the opinion that religion does not ordinarily leads to violence but rather happens as a result of several factors such as political, social, and ideological where religion becomes entangled with violent expressions of social aspirations, personal pride, and movement for political change. CS Lewis also suggested that religion involves faith or a belief that cannot be proven or disproven by sciences. A study in the United States involving college students found that majority of undergraduates in both natural and social sciences did not think there was conflict between science and religion. Another studies polled between 1981 and 2001 on views of science and religion showed that countries with higher religious values have stronger trust in science. The present arguments pit science against religion so let's take one very important aspect of science and evaluate how religion impacts human welfare. Let us take grief. Human grief from the scientific point view has both cognitive and neurochemical components. We mostly think on past moments, future lost, hopes dashed, memories decaying. Just like in all mammals, grief is a form of separation distress. The mammalian brains are hardwired for the calming comfort of a caregiver's touch, and when that is denied to human, especially permanently, the brain experience major reduction in opioids, oxytocin, and prolactin. Religious belief reduces the severity of that separation and religious practices develops, codify, and authenticate grieving customs that serve to offer a kind of emotional substitute for such loss. Both cognitively and affectively, religion helps us to cope with grief. This calming effect associated with religion has been observed among those who do not believe in religion especially when a dear one is hospitalised with critical illness. The non-believer of religion at a point engross him/her-self upon the divine intervention to help their loved ones. At that critical moment, both the believers and non-believers hopes depend on the Supreme Being.

Religion gives meaning and purpose to life. What readers must know is many things in life are difficult to understand; even with today's world of highly scientific advancement, certain things such as death remains a mystery and religious faith and belief can assist humanity to make sense of things that science cannot tell us. In addition, religion reinforces social unity and stability. Religion strengthens social stability in several ways including it gives people common set of beliefs which is an important agent for socialization and communal practices of religion brings people together physically which facilitates their communication and other social interaction thereby strengthening their social bonds. Religion is also a platform for social control and this facilitates social order. Religion teaches people moral behaviour which can help them to learn how to be good members of the society. Religion is also a greater source for psychological and physical well-being. Religious faith and practice can improve psychological well-being by being the source of comfort to people in times of distress and by improving their social interaction with others in places of worship. Several studies have shown that people of all ages are mostly happier and more satisfied with their lives if they are religious. Finally, religion may be a source of motivation for positive social change. For example, religion played significant role in the development of Southern civil rights movements' decades ago. Religious beliefs that were motivated by Malcolm X and Martin Luther King Jr.

One question that needs to be answered is does humanity need religion when we have significant scientific and human development? My sincere answer is YES. Humanity has lost it. We are now people of greed. We have lost focus. The world has lost its sense of humanity and we have completely lost direction. There is no doubt humanity has achieved significant development but that developments came with a cost: We have lost our identity. The world is now beleaguered by wars, unprecedented corruptions, and hatred. We have lost focus and cannot differentiate our sexual orientation. Humanity is in desperate state. We must recalibrate humanity to regain our morality. The best strategy for humanity is to follow divine laws which do not favour an individual. The world should not lose hope for Islam can provide solution that would recalibrate the world. Among all religions, it is Islam that gives us the optimism of hopefulness for Allah has shown us the strategy to create hope for lasting bliss both in this world and the eternal hereafter. It is known fact that life is full of highs and lows. In recent times when humanity has lost direction and every seconds life is becoming difficult. Allah has through Islam given us every reason to rely on Him and to hope for his interventions. Satan is busy using the weapon of despair so that human beings would turn away from Allah. Turning towards Allah is the best strategy for us to restore hope. Allah therefore says:

> **"I am just as My slave thinks I am, and I am with him if He remembers Me. If he remembers Me in himself, I too, remember him in Myself; and if he remembers Me in a group of people, I remember him in a better and nobler gathering (i.e. of Angels); and if he comes one span nearer to Me, I go one cubit nearer to him; and if he comes one cubit nearer to Me, I go a distance of two outstretched arms nearer to him; and if he comes to Me walking, I go to him running."**

Allah has therefore opened the door for us to turn to him and that no sin is big and thinks by turning to Satan who has turned the world upside. Allah's mercy is bigger than Satan's mechanisation.

The Prophet (SAW) advised us: *"Whoever persists in asking for pardon, Allah will grant him relief from every worry, and a way out from every hardship, and will grant him provision from (sources he could never imagine)."*

Allah called upon humanity to call on Him for assistance. The Prophet (SAW) therefore recommended a prayer for us: *"O Allah! I seek refuge with You from worry and grief, from incapacity and laziness, from cowardice and miserliness, from being heavily in debt and from being overpowered by (other) men."*

Life tribulation and trials are part of our daily life. At this period of desperation, we must remember that Allah (SWT) informed us in the Holy Quran:

"And we will surely test you with something of fear and hunger, some loss in wealth, lives and fruits (of your toil), but give glad tidings to those who patiently persevere.*"*

To the present and future, let us remember that Allah (SWT) has informed us that the result of hope is excellence. Possessing hope is a great attribute and this should motivate us to look for this excellence quality. We can learn a lot from the story of Prophet Yusuf (AS) who was sold by his brothers and imprisoned for false allegation. His father Yaqub (AS) was full of sorrow but never lost hope although Yusuf (AS) was gone for decades. From the story of Yusuf (AS) we can reason that Allah has plan. The challenges we are facing now as human beings are challenges that would make us better human beings.

To conclude, what do we take from COVID-19? This is a virus that even the naked eyes cannot see yet it completely brought the world to a standstill. Both economic and social life of human beings came to a complete stop. Those who are challenging Allah (SWT) should know that Allah (SWT) should not be disobeyed. Only one virus taught the world showed the power of Allah. We need to recalibrate human values to the Supreme and the religion that has the capability of doing that is Islam.

ETHICS AND MORALITY
OF THE QURAN

—————————————— ❖ ——————————————

Ethics refers to the principles of "good" vs. "evil" while morality refers to the sense of right and wrong that is normally accepted by a community. Although some western philosophers do not differentiate between morality and ethics, there are some differences. Morals are guidelines that affect individuals while ethics consist of guidelines that affect larger groups or communities. Ethics are therefore more culturally biased than morality. In this book, ethics and morality would be used interchangeable. Morality is divided into two types: descriptive and normative. In descriptive, morality is addressed from personal or culture values, code of conduct, or social mores from a society that provides these codes of conduct where it is applied and is accepted by an individual. It does not imply objective claims of right or wrong. Normative ethics on the other hand evaluates ethical behaviour which investigates questions regarding how one should act, in a moral manner. Western philosophers have been grouped into three groups on the basis of ethics: virtue ethics which hold the belief that being good is necessary for human to flourish, utilitarians who believes that good action leads to greatest happiness for the greatest, and the Kantians believes an action cannot be universalised (for e.g. you don't kill just because everybody is killing).

The Western moral philosophy began in the 4th and 5th century in Greece. As philosophers were exposed to different culture, questions were asked to differentiate between nature and convention as well as what is meant to be "just" in each case. As questions were being asked about morality and the best possible way to lead ethical life, more questions were asked; like "what constitute good life?" and "what do we really means when we refer to life as good?" These question raised more confusion resulting in some philosophers referring good life as eudemonia which was literally translated as "happiness" while others translated it as "objective human flourishing" Philosophers such as Plato, Aristotle and others all followed the eudemonistic type of ethics with different school of thought presenting different methodology of achieving this eudaimonia. Man is known to be naturally egoist who pursues his own self-interest even when it was detrimental to others. Therefore morality from human point of view is aimed at helping man achieve his goal no matter the price. Socrates told his friend Crito: "the most important thing isn't living, but living well." In Socrates' view, no one knowingly commit wrong. Committing wrong result in non fulfilment of eudemonia, thus no one would knowingly do so. Plato, on the other hand believed that justice is a kind of harmony between the three different parts of the just society which, corresponds to the individual's part of the soul, when a person achieves harmony between these parts, Plato thought they will naturally act justly in the conventional sense. But he added, they will be acting in their own interest because the just person is happier than the unjust. Aristotle in his argument wrote: "Every craft aims at some good."

The moral concept of the West is therefore based personhood where an individual is viewed as a priority and more fundamental than society, which is treated as artificial entity just to satisfy human needs. Therefore when the social order is not longer serving the necessary function, then it must be reorganized and redesigned to restore its function. Therefore, based on this concept, Western morality is based on the rights of individuals. Dworkin therefore argued that moral codes consist of personal rights, duties, and social goals but they may differ in the priority given to these three categories.

Western philosophers understanding of morality has led to complete and irreparable disintegration of moral values. The Western moral system promotes nakedness, sex, smoking, drug abuse, and no respect for authorities. In Africa which possess some of the perfect moral values, the infiltration of Western philosophers' type of morality has resulted in some people dressing like robots all in the name of western life thereby abandoning the rich Africa culture, girls as young as 8 years engaging in sex while the wealthy view women as sex toys for fun. The western type of morality is turning Africa boys to become sex beasts while girls dress and behave like prostitutes. Drug abuse is now becoming a global public health burden which can all be attributed to western type of moral value. This means the western type of morality should not have any place in global affairs.

The Quran contains about 159 verses that discuss morality and ethics for humanity. Considering these verses to be source of inspirations, all the verses would be listed in this book (below). The moral system that is thought by the Holy Quran does not only define morality but also guides the human race on how to achieve it, both individually and collectively.

It is only Islam that can provide the best platform to provide the moral and ethical lessons that the world urgently needs. These Quran-derived moral and ethical lessons cover all facets of human lives.

In Quran chapter 68 verse 4, Allah (SWT) had this for humanity:

> **"And most surely you conform (yourself) to sublime morality."**

In Quran 4:36, Allah advised humans:

> **"And worship Allah and associate not aught with Him; and unto patents show kindness, and also into kindred and orphans and the needy and the near neighbour and the distant neighbour and the companion by your side and the wayfarer and those whom your right hands own. Verily Allah loveth not one who is vainglorious, boaster."**

Moral teachings in the Quran

Below are some of the Quranic verses that provides lessons on morality.

- Respect and honour all human beings irrespective of their religion, colour, race, sex, language, status, property, birth, profession/job and so on ... [Quran:17:70]
- Talk straight, to the point, without any ambiguity or deception [Quran:33:70]

- Choose best words to speak and say them in the best possible way ... [Quran:17:53], [2:83]
- Do not shout. Speak politely keeping your voice low. [Quran: 31:19]
- Always speak the truth. Shun words that are deceitful and ostentatious: [Quran:22:30]
- Do not confound truth with falsehood ... [Quran:2:42]
- Say with your mouth what is in your heart ... [Quran:3:167]
- Speak in a civilised manner in a language that is recognised by the society and is commonly used ... [Quran:4:5]
- When you voice an opinion, be just, even if it is against a relative ... [Quran:6:152]
- Do not be a bragging boaster ... [Quran:31:18]
- Do not talk, listen or do anything vain ... [Quran:23:3], [Quran:28:55]
- Do not participate in any paltry. If you pass near a futile play, then pass by with dignity... [Quran: 25:72]
- Do not verge upon any immodesty or lewdness whether surreptitious or overt ... [Quran:6:151]
- If, unintentionally, any misconduct occurs by you, then correct yourself expeditiously ... [Quran:3:134]
- Do not be contemptuous or arrogant with people ... [Quran:31:18]
- Do not walk haughtily or with conceit ... [Quran:17:37], [Quran:31:18]
- Be moderate in thy pace ... [Quran:31:19]
- Walk with humility and sedateness ... [Quran:25:63]
- Keep your gazes lowered devoid of any lecherous leers and salacious stares ... [Quran:24:30],[Quran:24:31], [Quran:40:19]
- If you do not have complete knowledge about anything, better keep your mouth shut. You might think that speaking about something without full knowledge is a trivial matter. But it might have grave consequences.. [Quran:24:15], [Quran:24:!6]
- When you hear something malicious about someone, keep a favourable view about him/ her until you attain full knowledge about the matter. Consider others innocent until they are proven guilty with solid and truthful evidence ... [Quran:24:12], Quran:24:13]

- Ascertain the truth of any news, lest you smite someone in ignorance and afterwards repent of what you did ... [Quran:49:6]
- Do not follow blindly any information of which you have no direct knowledge. (Using your faculties of perception and conception) you must verify it for yourself. In the Court of your Lord, you will be held accountable for your hearing, sight, and the faculty of reasoning ... [Quran:17:36]
- Never think that you have reached the final stage of knowledge and nobody knows more than yourself. Remember! Above everyone endowed with knowledge is another endowed with more knowledge ...? [Quran: 12:76] ... Even the Prophet [SAW] was asked to keep praying, "O My sustainer! Advance me in knowledge." [Quran:20:114]
- The believers are but a single Brotherhood. Live like members of one family, brothers and sisters unto one another ... [Quran:49:10]
- Do not make mockery of others or ridicule others ... [Quran:49:11]
- Do not defame others [Quran:49:11]
- Do not insult others by nicknames [Quran:49:11]
- Avoid suspicion and guesswork. Suspicion and guesswork might deplete your communal energy [Quran:49:12]
- Spy not upon one another [Quran:49:12]
- Do not backbite one another [Quran:49:12]
- When you meet each other, offer good wishes and blessings for safety. One who conveys to you a message of safety and security and also when a courteous greeting is offered to you, meet it with a greeting still more courteous or (at least) of equal courtesy [Quran:4:86]
- When you enter your own home or the home of somebody else, compliment the inmates [Quran:24:61]
- Do not enter houses other than your own until you have sought permission; and then greet the inmates and wish them a life of blessing, purity and pleasure [Quran:24:27]
- Treat kindly Your parents, Relatives, The orphans" And those who have been left alone in the society [Quran:4:36]
- Take care of the needy, the disabled, those whose hard earned income is insufficient to meet their needs, And those whose

businesses have stalled, And those who have lost their jobs [Quran:4:36]

- Treat kindly Your related neighbours, and unrelated neighbours, Companions by your side in public gatherings, or public transportation.. [Quran:4:36]
- Be generous to the needy wayfarer, the homeless son of the street, and the one who reaches you in a destitute condition.. [Quran:4:36]
- Be nice to people who work under your care … [Quran:4:36]
- Do not follow up what you have given to others to afflict them with reminders of your generosity … [Quran:2:262]
- Do not expect a return for your good behaviour, not even thanks … [Quran:76:9]
- Cooperate with one another in good deeds and do not cooperate with others in evil and bad matters … [Quran:5:2]
- Do not try to impress people on account of self-proclaimed virtues … [Quran:53:32]
- You should enjoin right conduct on others but mend your own ways first. Actions speak louder than words. You must first practice good deeds yourself, and then preach … [Quran:2:44]
- Correct yourself and your families first before trying to correct others … [Quran:66:6]
- Pardon gracefully if anyone among you who commits a bad deed out of ignorance, and then repents and amends … [Quran:6:54], [Quran:3:134]
- Divert and sublimate your anger and potentially virulent emotions to creative energy, and become a source of tranquillity and comfort to people.. [Quran:3:134]
- Call people to the Way of your Lord with wisdom and beautiful exhortation. Reason with them most decently … [Quran:16:125]
- Leave to themselves those who do not give any importance to the Divine code and have adopted and consider it as mere play and amusement … [Quran:6:70]
- Sit not in the company of those who ridicule Divine Law unless they engage in some other conversation … [Quran:4:140]
- Do not be jealous of those who are blessed.. [Quran:4:54]
- In your collective life, make rooms for others … [Quran:58:11]

- When invited to dine, go at the appointed time. Do not arrive too early to wait for the preparation of meal or linger after eating to engage in bootless babble. Such things may cause inconvenience to the host [Quran:33:53]
- Eat and drink [what is lawful] in moderation.. [Quran:7:31]
- Do not squander your wealth senselessly … [Quran:17:26]
- Fulfil your promises and commitments … [Quran:17:34]
- Keep yourself clean, pure … [Quran:9:108]
- Dress-up in agreeable attire and adorn yourself with exquisite character from inside out … [Quran:7:26]
- Seek your provision only by fair endeavour … [Quran:29:17], [Quran:2:188]
- Do not devour the wealth and property of others unjustly, nor bribe the officials or the judges to deprive others of their possessions … [Quran:2:188]
- Do not be rude in speech (3:159)
- Restrain Anger (3:134)
- Be good to others (4:36)
- Do not be arrogant (7:13)
- Forgive others for their mistakes (7:199)
- Speak to people mildly (20:44)
- Lower your voice (31:19)
- Do not ridicule others (49:11)
- Be dutiful to parents(17:23)
- Do not say a word of disrespect to parents (17:23)
- Write down the debt (2:282)
- Do not follow anyone blindly (2:170)
- Grant more time to repay if the debtor is in hard time (2:280)
- Don't consume interest (2:275)
- Do not engage in bribery (2:188)
- Do not break the promise (2:177)
- Keep the trust (2:283)
- Do not mix the truth with falsehood (2:42)
- Appointment on merit, Judge with justice (4:58)
- Stand out firmly for justice (4:135)

- Wealth of the dead should be distributed among his family members (4:7)
- Women also have the right for inheritance (4:7)
- Do not devour the property of orphans (4:10)
- Protect orphans (2:220)
- Do not consume one another's wealth unjustly (4:29)
- Try for settlement between people (49:9)
- Avoid suspicion (49:12)
- Do not spy and backbite (2:283)
- Do not spy or backbite (49:12)
- Spend wealth in charity (57:7)
- Encourage feeding poor (107:3)
- Help those in need by finding them (2:273)
- Do not spend money extravagantly (17:29)
- Do not invalidate charity with reminders (2:264)
- Honour guests (51:26)
- Order righteousness to people only after practicing it yourself(2:44)
- Do not commit abuse on the earth (2:60)
- Do not prevent people from mosques (2:114)
- Fight only with those who fight you (2:190)
- Keep the etiquettes of war (2:191)
- Do not turn back in battle (8:15)
- No compulsion in religion (2:256)
- Believe in all prophets (2:285)
- Do not have sexual intercourse during menstrual period (2:222)
- Breast feed your children for two complete years (2:233)
- Do not even approach unlawful sexual intercourse (17:32)
- Choose rulers by their merit (4,58. 2:247)
- Do not burden a person beyond his scope (2:286)
- Do not become divided (3:103)
- Think deeply about the wonders and creation of this universe (3:191)
- Men and Women have equal rewards for their deeds (3:195)
- Do not marry those in your blood relation (4:23)
- Family should be led by men (4:34)
- Do not be miserly (4:37)

- Do not keep envy (4:54)
- Do not kill each other (4:92)
- Do not be an advocate for deceit (4:105)
- Do not cooperate in sin and aggression (5:2)
- Cooperate in righteousness (5:2)
- Having majority' is not a criterion of truth (6:116)
- Be just (5:8)
- Punish for crimes in an exemplary way (5:38)
- Strive against sinful and unlawful acts (5:63)
- Do not enter parents' private room without asking permission (24:58)
- Dead animals, blood, the flesh of swine are prohibited (5:3)
- Avoid intoxicants and alcohol (5:90)
- Do not gamble (5:90)
- Do not insult others' deities (6:108)
- Don't reduce weight or measure to cheat people (6:152)
- Eat and Drink, But Be Not Excessive (7:31)
- Wear good cloths during prayer times (7:31)
- Protect and help those who seek protection (9:6)
- Keep Purity (9:108)
- Never give up hope of Allah's Mercy (12:87)
- Allah will forgive those who have done wrong out of ignorance (16:119)
- Invitation to God should be with wisdom and good instruction (16:125)
- No one will bear others' sins (17:15)
- Do not kill your children for fear of poverty (17:31)
- Do not pursue that of which you have no knowledge (17:36)
- Keep aloof from what is vain (23:3)
- Do not enter others' houses without seeking permission (24:27)
- Allah will provide security for those who believe only in Allah (24:55)
- Walk on earth in humility (25:63)
- Do not neglect your portion of this world (28:77)
- Invoke not any other god along with Allah (28:88)
- Do not engage in homosexuality (29:29)
- Enjoin right, forbid wrong (31:17)

- Do not walk in insolence through the earth (31:18)
- Women should not display their finery (33:33)
- Allah forgives all sins (39:53)
- Do not despair of the mercy of Allah (39:53)
- Repel evil by good (41:34)
- Decide on affairs by consultation (42:38)
- Most noble of you is the most righteous (49:13)
- No Monasticism in religion (57:27)
- Those who have knowledge will be given a higher degree by Allah (58:11)
- Treat non-Muslims in a kind and fair manner (60:8)
- Save yourself from covetousness (64:16)
- Seek forgiveness of Allah. He is Forgiving and Merciful (73:20)

These verses are self-explanatory. A friend while I was working on this book suggested that there is nothing like religion but the so-called religions are just cultural manifestations and that what we (human beings) are missing are cultures that cannot be changed for the sake of the rich and that these cultures should be equal before every person irrespective of the status of the person. After I identified these verses, I sent a copy to him and he came back to me that with the comment "Islam has the best culture." The Holy Prophet (SAW) was described as the walking Quran that was why he (SAW) possessed the best quality of character as he (SAW) said: "*I have only been sent to perfect noble character/ conduct.*"

The companion Anas (RA) commenting about the character of the Holy Prophet (SAW) said: "I served him (SAW) for ten years, and he never said a word of displeasure to me, nor did he ever say to me concerning something I had done: Why did you do that? And he never said to me concerning what I had not done: Why did you not do this?" Another companion narrated that the Holy Prophet (SAW) said: "*Noble character will be the heaviest thing on a Muslim scale of good deeds on the Day of Resurrection. Allah detests the rude and foul-mouthed.*" All these point to one direction: ethics and moral values are held in high esteem in the Holy Quran. The moral system of Islam as outlined in the verses above encompasses all facet of human life. We are in an era where good and evil are regarded as relative concepts. However, in Islam, good and evil are not regarded as relative but the global standard by which actions are judged whether moral or immoral. While defining morality, the Holy Quran also prescribed how these moral values can be achieved. Perfect example is the verses below:

> **"It is not righteousness that ye turn your faces Towards east or West; but it is righteousness- to believe in Allah and the Last Day, and the Angels, and the Book, and the Messengers; to spend of your substance, out of love for Him, for your kin, for orphans, for the needy, for the wayfarer, for those who ask, and for the ransom of slaves; to be steadfast in prayer, and practice regular charity; to fulfil the contracts which ye have made; and to be firm and patient, in pain (or suffering) and adversity, and throughout all periods of panic. Such are the people of truth, the Allah-fearing." [Al-Qur'an 2:177]**

> **Say: the things that my Lord hath indeed forbidden are: shameful deeds, whether open or secret; sins and trespasses against truth or reason; assigning of partners to Allah, for which He hath given no authority; and saying things about Allah of which ye have no knowledge. [Al-Qur'an 7:33]**

> **"The Day whereon neither wealth nor sons will avail, but only he (will prosper) that brings to Allah a sound heart" [Al-Quran: 26:88-89]**

Moral system in Islam therefore covers every facets of human's life, from greetings to international relations. It even covers how we should deal with animals, the environment, etc. In essence, the Holy Quran promotes that human being should not only be morally healthy, but must also contribute to the moral values of the society as a whole. Failure to do this means an individual is immoral and immorality means evil in the words of the western moral system! The Holy Prophet (SAW) gave summarized the moral system as follows:

1. to remain conscious of God,
2. whether in private or in public;
3. to speak justly, whether angry or pleased;
4. to show moderation both when poor and when rich,
5. to reunite friendship with those who have broken off with me;
6. to give to him who refuses me;
7. that my silence should be occupied with thought;
8. that my looking should be an admonition; and that
9. I should command what is right.

Islam has provided the spiritual and moral lessons which humanity urgently needs at this crucial moment when humanity has completely lost direction and just clinging on the rope of hope. This rope of hope is delusional if we are to follow the standard set by Western Philosophy because as is all human ideologies, there are bound to be human errors. It is only the spiritual guidance that can liberate humanity from the clutches of social and moral vices that has completely taking over from humanity.

REFERENCES

1. 10 Quotations by Western scholar on Prophet Muhammad on https://islamexplained.info/2019/08/24/western-scholars-on-prophet-muhammad/ (Accessed on 08/12/2023).

2. Asad, Talal. 2003. Formations of the secular: Christianity, Islam, Modernity, Stanford: Stanford University Press

3. Bible bombshell? Jesus Christ was NOT crucified according to ancient 'Gospel of Barnabas' on https://www.express.co.uk/news/weird/1097620/bible-news-discovery-jesus-christ-crucifixion-truth-book-of-barnabas (Assessed on 03/01/2024)

4. Brooks A: Religious faith and charitable giving on https://www.hoover.org/publications/policy-review (Accessed on 24/10/2024)

5. Brown Jonathan AC (2014): Misquoting Muhammad: The challenge and choices of interpreting the Prophet's legacy; Oneworld Publications

6. Al-Kafi volume 1-3

7. Bailey, David. What are the merits of recent claims by atheistic scholars that modern science proves religion to be false on http://www.sciencemeetsreligion.org/theology/atheists.php (Accessed 24/10/2024)

8. Carley Bruce (2022): The end of monogamy? An explanation of non-monogamous relationship dynamics, Canada J of Family and Truth; DOI: 10.29173/cjfy29769.

9. Christopher Kaczor. Why governments haven't and shouldn't recognize polygamy, April 26 2016 on https://www.thepublicdiscourse.com/2016/04/16666/ (Accessed on 07/12/2023)

10. Christopher PS (2011): US College students'perception of religion and science: conflict, collaboration, or independence? A research note, J for the Scientific study of religion, 50: 175-186

11. Conesa-Sevilla, J: Apostasy in 21st century academia: Religion-politics in America's higher education on

12. Conley TD, Ziegler A, et al (2012): A critical examination of popular assumption about the benefit and outcomes of monogamous relationship, Personality and Social Psychology Review; DOI: 10.1177/1088868312467087.

13. Deeb, Lara, 2006. An Enchantment Modern: Gender and Public Piety in Shi'I Lebanon. Princeton Studies in Muslim Politics. Princeton: Princeton University Press

14. Fitzgerald Timothy (2000): The ideology of Religious Studies, new York: Oxford University Press (Published 2003)

15. Harris, Sam (2005): The End of Faith. WW Norton & Company

16. Hastings, James (1909): Encyclopaedia of religion and ethics, volume 2 on https://archive.org/details/in.ernet.dli.2015.56055/page/190/mode/1up (Accessed on 24/10/2024)

17. Hwang K-K (2015). Morality 'East' and 'West/: Cultural concerns. In James D Wright (editor-in-chief), International Encyclopaedia of the Social & Behavioral Sciences, 2nd edition, Vol 15. Oxford: Elsevier. Pp.806-810.

18. Hikmat Sharquiyah: Looking at a Muslim's responsibility towards others. September 8, 2014 on https://www.mindanews.com (Accessed on 13/12/2023)

19. Jamil M, Abbas SZ, et al (2023): Islam teachings and religious brotherhood in the Islamic society, HTS Theological Studies; DOI; 10.4102/hts.v7911.8369

20. John Witt, Jr. The Western Case for monogamy and polygamy, Cambridge University Press, New York and Cambridge, 2015.

21. Jonathan AC Brown: Misquoting Muhammad, The challenges and choices of interpreting the Prophet's legacy, One world; 2014.

22. Juergensmeyer, Mark (2001): Terror in the mind of God: The global rise of religious violence: Updated edition University of California Press

23. Kabbani H, seraj H, Ahmad H (2006): Jihad- A misunderstood concept from Islam on https://web.archive.org/web/200606271 31412/http://www.sunnah.org/fiqh/jihad_judicial_ruling.htm (Accessed on 24/10/2024)

24. Kerley, Kent R; Matthews, Todd L, Blanchard Troy C (2005): Relgiosity, religious participation, and negative prison behaviours, J for the Scientific Study of Religion; 44: 443-457

25. Lucretius T: Stanford Encyclopaedia on https://archive.org/details/in.ernet.dli.2015.56055/page/190/mode/1up (Accessed 24/10/2024)

26. The Prophet was a seeker of truth: Mahatma Gandhi on https://timesofindia.indiatimes.com/city/ahmedabad/the-prophet-was-a-seeker-of-truth-bapu/articleshow/55929973.cms (Accessed on 08/12/2023)

27. The Quran, An English translation of the meaning of the Quran, Checked and revised by Mahmud Y Zayid, Dar Al-Choura Beirut, Lebanon

28. Regnerus MD, Burdette A (2006): Religious change and adolescent family dynamics; The Sociological Qtr; 47: 175-194

29. Salim bin Muhammad. 1999. Muhammad, the Beloved of Allah. Darussalam, Kingdom of Saudi Arabia

30. Saroglou V, Pichon I, et al (2005): Prosocial behavoir and religion: New evidence based on projective measures and peer ratings, J for the Scientific Study of Religion; 44: 323-348

31. Mansoureh Ebrahimi & Kamaruzaman Yusoff (2017): Islamic identity, ethical principles and human values, Eur J of Multidisciplinary Studies, 6: 326-337

32. Medieval Christian's views on Muhammad on https://en.wikipedia.org/wiki/Medieval_Christian_views_on_Muhammad (Accessed on 30/11/2023).

33. Mohd Irwan Syazli Saidin. 2018. Revolution in the contemporary Muslim world: Review of the 1979 Iran's revolution and the 2011 Arab uprising. Malaysia J of History, Politics and strategies. 45: 104-125

34. Morris A (1984): The origins of the civil rights movement: Black communities organizing for change. New York, NY: Free Press

35. Mittermaier. Amira. 2019. Giving to God: Islamic Charity in Revolutionary Times. Berkeley: University of California Press

36. Murray Evan D, Cunningham Milles G, Price Bruce H (2011): The role of psychotic disorders in religious history considered J of Neuropsychiatry and Clinical Neurosciences; 24: 410-426

37. Onfray, Michel (2007): Atheist Manifesto: The Case against Christianity, Judaism, and Islam, Arcade Publishing

38. Osman Tarek, 2017. A history of political Islam from the fall of Othman empire to the rise of ISIS. New Heaven: Yale University Press.

39. Quran: All Quranic verses about Jesus, January 3, 2022 on https://www.getquranic.com/all-quranic-verses-about-jesus/ (Accessed on 03/01/2024).

40. Rasmussen KB, March 1, 2009 on https://www.jstor.org/stable/resrept13162 (Accessed on 16/12/2023).

41. Robert T Wise: Merely a line in the sand: A model for Christian-Muslim Dailogue, March 1, 2014 on reformedjournal.com (Accessed on 06/12/2023).

42. Taylor Christopher, July 2019. "Reflections on the theory of Zaakat" Allegra Lab.

43. The New Atheists, Internet Encyclopaedia of Philosophy on https://iep.utm.edu/n-atheis/ (Accessed 24/10/2024)

44. The Oxford Handbook on Atheism (2016) Oxford University Press

45. The Sustainable Development Goals Report 2023: Special Edition on https://unstats.un.org/sdgs/report/2023/?_gl=1*oig6n8*_ga*M TUxMjg4NDAxNS4xNzA1NzY3NDc0*_ga_TK9BQL5X7Z*M TcwNTc2NzQ3NC4xLjAuMTcwNTc2NzQ3NC4wLjAuMA. (Accessed on 20/01/2024).

46. Seyed Hossein Mousavian. 2023. A revolution and A war: How Iran transformed today's Middle East, The Cairo Review of Global Affairs.

47. Uecker JE (2008): Religious and spiritual responses to 9/11: Evidence from the Add health study, Sociol Spectr; 28: 477-509

48. Voltaire's Philosophical Dictionary on https://history.hanover.edu/texts/voltaire/volrelig.html (Accessed 24/10/2024)

49. Walter Sinnott-Armstrong, Thalia Wheatley (2012): The disunity of morality and why it matters to philosophy, The Monist; 95: 355=377.

50. Ward, Keith (2006): Is religion dangerous? London: Lion Hudson Plc: Lion

Websites

- https://quransubjects.wordpress.com/2019/12/03/ethics-morality-quran-99-verses/ ..
- https://www.whyislam.org/social-ties-2/morality-ethics-in-islam/ ..
- https://quransubjects.wordpress.com/2019/12/03/ethics/

Milton Keynes UK
Ingram Content Group UK Ltd.
UKHW030710051124
450766UK00001B/271

9 798823 088947